TO *Baby* WITH *Love*

TO Baby WITH Love

35 GORGEOUS GIFTS TO MAKE FOR BABIES AND TODDLERS

Deborah Schneebeli-Morrell

CICO BOOKS

LONDON NEW YORK

To Luna Luz and Florez Sun

Published in 2011 by CICO Books
An imprint of Ryland Peters & Small Ltd
20–21 Jockey's Fields,
London WC1R 4BW
519 Broadway, 5th Floor
New York, NY 10012

www.cicobooks.com

10 9 8 7 6 5 4 3 2 1

Text and project designs © Deborah
Schneebeli-Morrell 2011
Design and photography © CICO Books
2011

A CIP catalog record for this book is
available from the Library of Congress
and the British Library.

ISBN 978 1 90756 313 3

Printed in China

Editor: **Alison Wormleighton**
Designer: **Elizabeth Healey**
Illustrator: **Kate Simunek**
Photographer: **Emma Mitchell**
ylist: **Sania Pell**

Contents

Introduction

The arrival of a new baby is a magical occasion, a time of celebration for the parents, family, and friends. What better way to express your joy and to welcome the new baby than with a special gift you have made yourself? A homemade, one-of-a-kind present is always appreciated and is much nicer to receive, and to give, than a store-bought gift. This book contains many useful and beautiful items that you can make at the time of the birth and throughout those adorable early years.

If you have always made and sewn things, then this lovely time is an opportunity for you to become even more creative, and you will find many inspiring projects in these pages. But even if you are new to sewing, there are still many simple and inventive gifts that the book will enable you to make.

The 35 projects range from the practical to the whimsical. In most cases they can be adapted if you wish, using different colors, fabrics, sizes, shapes, or designs. And if you don't have a sewing machine, you could sew them by hand instead, since most of the items are small.

Many of the projects use fabric scraps, so if you like patchwork or appliqué and have accumulated a collection of fabrics, then this is the book for you. Most of the items are quick and easy to make, and also inexpensive, yet the resulting gift is likely to be cherished throughout childhood and may even go on to become a family heirloom.

Deborah Schneebeli-Morrell

CHAPTER ONE

NEW BABY

★ SUMMER QUILT ★ BIRD MOBILE ★ CATTY STUFFED TOY ★ PORTABLE CHANGING MAT ★ WINTER QUILT ★ OWL CRIB DECORATION ★ CRIB MUSIC BOX ★ HEARTS AND POMPOMS GARLAND ★ APPLIQUÉ PHOTO ALBUM ★ BATH-TIME WASHCLOTH ★ CARRYALL BAG FROM VINTAGE FABRIC

Summer quilt

THIS PRETTY REVERSIBLE QUILT IS MADE FROM SMALL SCRAPS OF
DRESS FABRIC. I USED TWO FAVORITE DRESSES SAVED FROM MY OWN
DAUGHTER'S CHILDHOOD TO CREATE AN HEIRLOOM WITH SPECIAL FAMILY
SIGNIFICANCE. THE PATTERNED FABRICS ARE FINE COTTON, SEWN ONTO
A SOLID PINK COTTON CHAMBRAY BACKGROUND. COTTON BATTING IS
SANDWICHED BETWEEN THE FRONT AND BACK, AND A SIMPLE RUNNING
STITCH SEWN THROUGH THE THREE LAYERS CREATES THE QUILTED
EFFECT. THIS MAKES A 20½ x 29IN (52 x 73CM) QUILT, BUT YOU
COULD ADJUST THE DIMENSIONS IF YOU WISH.

1 For the patches on the quilt
front, cut out three 6in (15cm)
squares from each of the two
floral fabrics, making six
squares in total.

2 For the backing fabric of the quilt front, cut
out a 22½ x 31in (57 x 78cm) rectangle from the
cotton chambray (adjusting the dimensions if
you wish) and then
turn under and press
a 1in (2.5cm) hem
all around.

You will need

- ★ Scraps of two fine cotton fabrics
  in floral prints

- ★ ⅔ yd (60cm) of cotton chambray
  in a solid color

- ★ Contrasting thread for basting

- ★ Cotton sewing thread to match
  chambray

- ★ Large scraps of polka-dot cotton
  fabric

- ★ Bleached cotton batting, usually
  available as a 45 x 60in (114 x
  152cm) piece

- ★ Pearl cotton embroidery thread,
  such as DMC size 5, in two colors

3 Turn under a ¼ in (5mm) hem all around each of the floral squares, basting the hems in place if you wish. Position the squares, right side up and equally spaced, on the front of the cotton chambray rectangle. Baste in place. Slipstitch neatly around all four edges of each square. Remove the basting, and press.

4 For the quilt back, cut enough pieces from the two floral fabrics and the polka-dot fabric to join into a rectangle that is the same size as the front, allowing an extra ⅜ in (1cm) all around each piece for seams. The size and quantity of the pieces will depend on your fabric scraps, but the easiest method is to cut enough rectangles of the same depth to join into one strip as long as the width of the quilt front. Pin adjacent rectangles with right sides together along one side edge and stitch a ⅜ in (1cm) seam, repeating until the strip is the correct length. Make more strips in the same way, varying the depth if you wish, but making the strips all the same length. Because the fabric isn't bulky, you can press the seam allowances to one side, which gives extra strength. Now join the strips together in the same way, so that the resulting rectangle is the size of the quilt front. (If the edges are uneven, trim them and restitch the ends of any seams that have been cut off.)

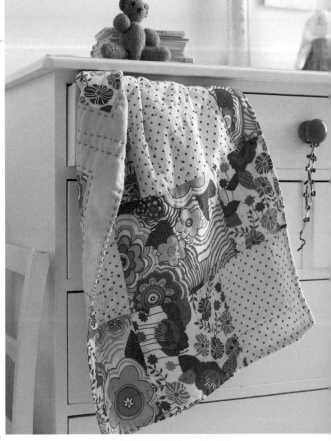

5 Cut out a rectangle of batting that is the same size as the front, less 1in (2.5cm) all around. Place the quilt front wrong side up on your work surface, and position the batting exactly in the center. Baste the two layers together loosely. Turn the quilt front over so it is right side up. Place the quilt back on top, right sides together. Baste and then machine stitch a 1in (2.5cm) seam around the edges, leaving an opening in the seam at the bottom edge. (You will be stitching close to the batting but not through it.)

6 Turn the quilt right side out; press. Turn in the edges of the opening, pin, and slipstitch the opening closed. Using the pearl cotton embroidery thread and an embroidery needle, sew running stitch around three similar squares on the front with one color of thread, and around the remaining three squares with the other color of thread. Sew more running stitch around the edge of the quilt, and finally sew a double line, one in each color, between the squares. Remove basting.

Bird mobile

MOBILES ARE POPULAR GIFTS FOR BABIES, AND BY MAKING YOUR OWN YOU CAN CHOOSE NICE, SOFT COLORS AND APPEALING MATERIALS. DESIGNED TO HANG ABOVE A CRIB, THIS PRETTY FABRIC MOBILE HAS FOUR LITTLE PATCHWORK BIRDS THAT WILL GENTLY MOVE AND CATCH THE BABY'S EYE. THE BIRDS ARE ATTACHED TO A METAL RING USING FINE RIBBONS, WHICH ARE EASY TO ADJUST.

You will need

★ Scraps of four linen or cotton fabrics in solid pink tones

★ Pattern for bird (see page 142)

★ Scraps of four cotton fabrics in patterns such as stripes and checks

★ Contrasting thread for basting

★ Sewing thread to match solid pink scraps

★ Polyester toy stuffing

★ Strong thread, for sewing on buttons

★ 12 small buttons: three in each of four colors (I used blue, violet, pearl, and fawn)

★ Two 40 x 1in (100 x 2.5cm) strips of pink cotton fabric

★ Double-sided tape

★ Metal ring about 10in (26cm) in diameter (bought from a florist's shop or cut from an old lampshade)

★ 1yd (1m) of satin ribbon ⅛in (3mm) wide, in each of four colors (I used pinks and violets), for attaching birds to ring

★ About 6–8yd (6–8m) of satin ribbon, depending on ceiling height, for attaching ring to ceiling

★ 1 cup hook

1 Fold the four pink scraps in half and draw around the bird pattern on each. Cut them out, to make eight bird shapes.

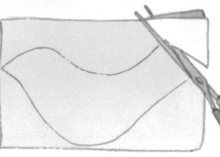

2 Fold the four patterned fabrics in half and draw a wing shape on each. Cut them out, to make eight wing pieces. Turn under a narrow hem all around each wing; baste the hem in place if you wish.

3 Place a wing, right side up, on the right side of one bird shape. Baste in place and slipstitch inconspicuously around the wing to secure. Remove basting. Sew the matching wing to the other side of the bird in the same way. Repeat for the other birds.

4 Pin the bird front to the bird back with right sides together. Machine stitch a ¼in (5mm) seam around the edge, leaving the tail end unstitched. Snip into the seam allowance on the curves, and snip off the point of the seam allowance at the beak. Turn the bird right side out, and press. Repeat for the other birds.

5 Fill each bird loosely with stuffing through the opening. To create a more three-dimensional shape, pull the front and back apart at the opening, aligning the top and bottom edges instead, with the stitched seam lines in the center. Turn in ¼in (5mm) along the top and bottom edges and slipstitch the opening closed.

6 Use strong thread to sew a pair of small buttons in the eye position on either side of each bird's head, sewing through the bird's head to attach the two buttons simultaneously. Finish by winding the thread behind the buttons and securing tightly before cutting.

7 To create a fringe on each of the two long pink strips, make closely spaced snips along one long edge at right angles to it, stopping each snip about ¼in (5mm) from the opposite edge. Wrap a little double-sided tape around the ring in one place, attach one end of the fringe to the tape, and wind the fringe tightly around half of the ring. Secure the end with tape. Do the same with the other strip so that the whole ring is covered.

8 To attach a bird to the ring, thread a tapestry needle with a 1yd (1m) length of ribbon, insert the needle through a button that matches the eyes, and then insert it into the base of the bird and up through the body. Take the ribbon over the ring and back down through the bird and button. Adjust the length and then tie a double knot in the ends of the ribbon to secure. Trim, leaving 1½in (4cm) ends. Neatly sew the ribbon in place where it touches the ring. Attach the other three birds in the same way, spacing them evenly around the ring and adjusting the length of the ribbons so that the birds are suspended at different heights.

9 To hang the ring from the ceiling, cut four pieces of ribbon, each long enough to reach the ceiling plus about 4in (10cm). Tie one end of each to the ring, spacing them evenly, and tie the other end of each in a loop, making sure the ribbons are all the same length. Insert a hook in the ceiling, and slide the loops onto the hook.

Catty stuffed toy

GIVE THIS DARLING LITTLE STUFFED CAT TO A NEWBORN BABY AND THEY ARE CERTAIN TO BECOME FRIENDS FOR LIFE. IT IS MADE FROM THE SOFTEST MATERIAL IN THREE SHADES OF PINK—I USED SOME OLD CASHMERE SWEATERS AND A COMFY OLD SHAWL, WHICH HAD FELTED SLIGHTLY IN THE WASH. THE FACE IS STITCHED WITH APPLIQUÉD WOOLEN PIECES FOR THE EYES AND THE NOSE, WHILE THE OTHER FEATURES ARE CREATED WITH SIMPLE WOOL EMBROIDERY, MAKING THIS A VERY SAFE TOY FOR A YOUNG BABY.

You will need

★ *Patterns for cat head, body, arms, and legs (see page 134)*

★ *Scraps of soft wool, such as cashmere or lamb's-wool, in three shades of one color*

★ *Sewing thread to match*

★ *Polyester toy stuffing*

★ *Contrasting thread for basting*

★ *Scraps of knitted wool in blue and rust for the eyes and nose*

★ *Crewel yarn in pink*

1 Using the patterns, cut out one body piece (for the front) from one piece of wool (I used the shawl), and cut out one head piece, two arm pieces, two leg pieces and a second body piece (for the back) from another shade of wool. Cut two more arm pieces, two more leg pieces, and another head piece from a third shade.

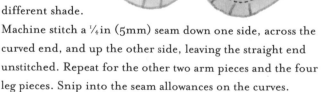

2 With right sides together, pin one arm piece to another in a different shade. Machine stitch a ¼ in (5mm) seam down one side, across the curved end, and up the other side, leaving the straight end unstitched. Repeat for the other two arm pieces and the four leg pieces. Snip into the seam allowances on the curves.

3 Turn both arms and both legs right side out. Loosely fill them with the polyester stuffing.

4 With right sides together, pin the short edge of the back body piece to the straight edge of a head piece in a different shade. Stitch a ³⁄₈ in (1cm) seam. Repeat to join the front body piece to the other head piece.

5 Place the stuffed arms, pointing inward, on the right side of the back body. The side of each arm that is the same shade as the back body should be on top. The unstitched ends of the arms should be even with the side edges of the back. Stitch in place at the sides.

6 Baste the front to the back, with right sides together, sandwiching the arms in between. Machine stitch a ³⁄₈ in (1cm) seam around the side and top edges, leaving the bottom edge open. (Be careful not to catch a paw in the opposite seam.) Remove the basting. Turn right side out.

7 Place the legs on the right side of the front, with the unstitched ends even with the lower edge of the front, and the feet near the neck. The side of each leg that is a different shade from the body back should be on top. Baste the legs to the lower edge of the front and then machine stitch them ¼ in (5mm) from the edge, sewing through the legs and the front only (not through the back). Remove the basting.

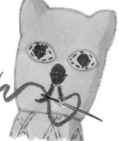

8 Stuff the head and body, distributing the stuffing evenly. Return the legs to the normal position. Turn under the ¼ in (5mm) seam allowance on the front and ends of the legs, and turn under the same amount on the back; pin. Slipstitch the back to the back of each leg and to the front along these edges.

9 For the eyes, cut out two almond shapes from the blue knitted wool and two smaller ovals from the rust knitted wool, and for the nose cut out an oval from the rust knitted wool. Sew the blue eyes in place with the crewel yarn and an embroidery needle, using running stitch around the edge of each. Sew the rust oval to each blue eye using a cross, bringing the needle up through the center with each stitch. Sew the nose in place with a cross in the same way.

10 Make the cat's mouth by embroidering the two curves in stem stitch (see Crib Music Box, step 2, page 36) using the crewel yarn.

Portable changing mat

THERE IS NO DOUBT THAT ONE OF THE MOST USEFUL PIECES OF BABY EQUIPMENT IS THE PORTABLE BABY-CHANGING MAT, ALLOWING ALL MANNER OF SURFACES TO BE BROUGHT INTO SERVICE COMFORTABLY AND HYGIENICALLY. NOT ONLY IS THIS CHANGING MAT SIMPLE TO MAKE, BUT IT CAN ALSO BE ROLLED UP AND FASTENED INTO A COMPACT, LIGHTWEIGHT FORM. THE INSIDE IS MADE FROM A PATCHWORK OF STRIPED T-SHIRT FABRICS, INTERLINED WITH POLYESTER BATTING AND WITH A BACKING OF PURPLE SEERSUCKER. ALTHOUGH SOME READY-MADE CHANGING MATS HAVE A PLASTIC SURFACE OR INTERLINING, THIS MAT IS ENTIRELY WASHABLE AND SO IT IS NOT NECESSARY TO USE WIPEABLE MATERIAL. THE FINISHED MAT IS 21 x 15½IN (53 x 40CM).

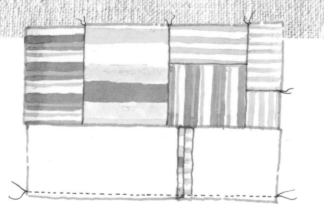

You will need

★ Five children's T-shirts in a selection of stripes

★ Sewing thread to match fabric for back

★ One 17 x 23in (44 x 57cm) piece of fabric for backing (I used purple seersucker)

★ One 16 x 21in (40 x 53cm) piece of polyester batting

★ Contrasting thread for basting

★ Matte embroidery cotton, size 4

1 Cut panels from the front and back of each T-shirt. Cut these into different-sized rectangles and stitch them together to make strips of patchwork (see Summer Quilt, step 4, page 12), arranging the stripes so that they run both vertically and horizontally. I used seven strips to make the mat. Press the seams open. With right sides together, join the strips with ⅜in (1cm) seams, to make the front of the mat. Press these seams open, too. Trim the edges so they are even and the patchwork is 17in (44cm) square.

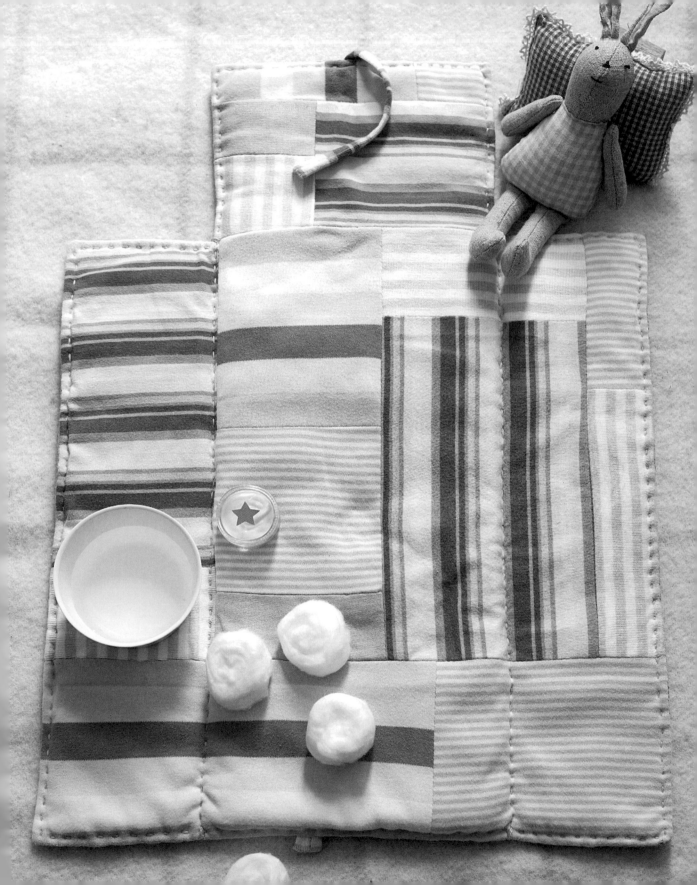

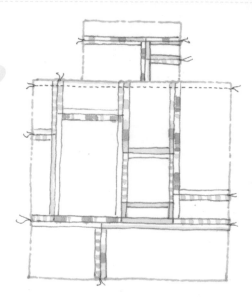

2 In the same way, make another patchwork for the head section, which should be 9 x 7in (23 x 17cm). Press all the seams open. With right sides together, pin one long edge of the head section to the center of one edge of the main section. Stitch a ¾in (2cm) seam; press the head section and the seam allowances away from the main section.

3 Trim the backing fabric so it is the same shape and size as the front of the mat, including the head section. Cut the batting so it is the same shape but is ¾in (2cm) smaller all around. Center the batting on the wrong side of the backing fabric; baste.

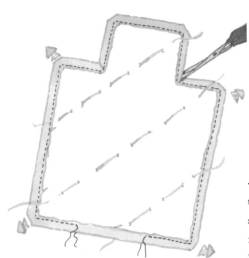

4 Pin the back to the front with right sides together and raw edges even. Stitch a ¾in (2cm) seam all around, leaving an opening in the lower edge. Snip off the seam allowances at the outer corners and clip into the seam allowances at the inner corners between the main section and the head.

5 Turn the mat right side out and press. Turn in the seam allowances on the opening, pin, and slipstitch the opening closed. Using the matte embroidery cotton and an embroidery needle, hand sew a line of running stitch all around the edge of the mat. Extend the lines of running stitch that are at either side of the head piece so they continue down the main part of the mat, keeping the lines equidistant from the side edges. Remove basting.

6 For the two ties, cut two 8½ x 1½in (21 x 4cm) strips of T-shirt material. Fold each in half lengthwise, right sides together, and machine stitch a ¼in (5mm) seam along the long edge. Trim the seam allowances to ⅛in (3mm). Turn right side out—it is useful to use a loop turner or a "quick unpick" tool. Iron each tie flat, with the seam running down the center. Tuck in the raw edges on the ends of each tie; slipstitch.

7 On the back of the mat, sew one tie to the center of the top of the head section. To find the position of the other tie, fold in the sides of the mat along the hand-stitched lines, and then roll up the mat, starting at the bottom. Sew the second tie to the back at the point where it meets the tie on the head section.

Winter quilt

WITH ITS SOFT WOOL TOP AND SILK LINING, HELD TOGETHER BY KNOTTED SILK RIBBONS, THIS LUXURIOUS QUILT IS COZY, COMFORTING, AND TACTILE. THE SIMPLE PATCHWORK IS MADE FROM PIECES OF FINE OLD SWEATERS AND A SHAWL, FROM MY COLLECTION OF GARMENTS MADE FROM FINE WOOL, CASHMERE, LAMB'S-WOOL, OR ANGORA. MOST PEOPLE HAVE AT LEAST ONE SWEATER LIKE THIS, PERHAPS SADLY DISCARDED BECAUSE IT HAS THE ODD MOTH HOLE. ONCE YOU LET YOUR FRIENDS KNOW THAT YOU ARE COLLECTING FOR A QUILT, YOU WILL BE SURPRISED AND DELIGHTED BY THE NUMBER OF USEFUL DONATIONS. THIS QUILT IS 24 x 32IN (60 x 80CM), BUT YOU COULD ADJUST THE SIZE IF YOU WISH.

You will need

★ Pieces (including ribbing from collars and cuffs) from several old woolen sweaters and a knitted wool shawl, in various tones (I used pinks, greens, and turquoise)

★ Sewing thread to match

★ One 24 x 32in (60 x 80cm) piece of polyester batting

★ Contrasting thread for basting

★ One 28 x 36in (70 x 90cm) piece of silk for lining

★ 1yd (1m) each of silk ribbons ³⁄₈in–⁵⁄₈in (1–1.5cm) wide in three colors (I used turquoise, pink, and pale pink)

★ Silk thread to match lining

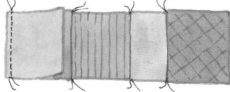

2 Lay out the pieces on your work surface to make sure you are happy with the arrangement, and adjust as necessary. With right sides together, pin each piece to the adjacent one in the block or strip, and machine stitch a ⅜in (1cm) seam, repeating until all the pieces are joined into strips. Because this fabric is quite bulky, press each seam open. Now pin each strip to the adjacent one with right sides together, and machine stitch a ⅜in (1cm) seam. Press the seams open.

1 Plan the patchwork design of squares and rectangles before you cut out the fabric. It will be easiest to sew pieces of the same depth into a strip, and make several strips of the same length which you can then stitch together relatively quickly. (A few small pieces can also be joined into a block of the same depth as the larger pieces that will form a strip. The block is then treated as a single piece.) The patchwork will need to be 24 x 32in (60 x 80cm), and each piece should have a ⅜in (1cm) seam allowance all around. Plan for some of the pieces to be turned so the grain is at right angles to other pieces—this looks especially good with pieces of ribbing. Now cut out the squares and rectangles from the woolen garments.

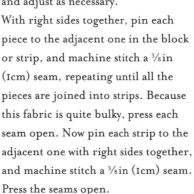

3 If the edges of the patchwork are uneven, trim them to make them straight, and so that the patchwork is 24 x 32in (60 x 80cm). Wherever you have had to trim off the ends of seams, machine stitch them again so that they will not unravel later.

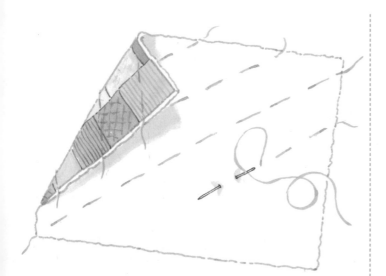

4 With the patchwork wrong side up on the work surface, lay the piece of batting on top of it, with the edges even. Secure over the whole surface with large basting stitches.

5 Lay the piece of silk, wrong side up, on the work surface and place the patchwork and batting centrally on top, patchwork side up. The silk should extend beyond the patchwork by 2in (5cm) all around. Thread one of the ribbons through a tapestry needle. At some of the joints of the seams in the wool, sew the ribbon through all three layers, tying it into a double knot on the patchwork front and trimming to leave ends 1½in (4cm) long. Repeat for the other colors of ribbons. You don't need too many ties, but try to space them evenly. Iron the ribbons flat.

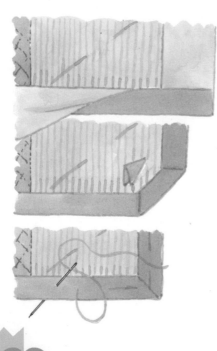

6 On each edge, fold the silk border in half lengthwise so the raw edge abuts the edge of the patchwork; press this first hem with a cool iron using a press cloth. Fold the hem over again, onto the patchwork, forming a border 1in (2.5cm) wide; press this second hem in the same way. To miter each corner, unfold the second hem on adjacent sides, leaving the first hem still folded. Fold the corner diagonally so that the creases of the unfolded hem are aligned; trim off the triangle between these creases. Now refold the second hem on each side, forming a miter at the corner. Baste the hems and miters in place.

7 Slipstitch the silk border to the patchwork, using silk thread and tiny stitches. (Slipstitch is useful for inconspicuously sewing a folded edge to a flat piece, as here, or two folded edges together, as for an opening in a seam. Bring the needle out through the folded edge and then, $\frac{1}{16}$ in (1–2mm) farther along, either insert it in the flat piece, picking up only a few threads, or insert it in the other fold and bring it out from the fold $\frac{1}{4}$ in (5mm) along. Continue in this way along the hem or opening.) Also slipstitch the miters. Remove basting.

Owl crib decoration

THESE CHARMING TWIN OWLS ARE A FRIENDLY PRESENCE KEEPING A WATCHFUL EYE OVER YOUR CHILD. BABIES LOVE MOVEMENT AND AS THESE OWLS SWING GENTLY, YOUR BABY WILL ATTEMPT TO CATCH AND HOLD THEM—A DEVELOPMENTAL MILESTONE. THE OWLS ARE MADE FROM RECYCLED T-SHIRTS, ALTHOUGH ANY SMOOTH, STRETCHY MATERIAL WILL DO. THE LONG STRAP THAT JOINS THE OWLS TOGETHER SHOULD ALWAYS BE LOOPED OVER THE TOP BAR OF THE CRIB OR THE HANDLE OF YOUR BABY CARRIER, SO ADJUST THE LENGTH OF THIS STRAP TO SUIT WHERE YOU WILL BE USING IT.

You will need

★ Patterns for owl body and face
(see page 135)

★ Scraps of T-shirt material in
fawn, green, and white

★ Contrasting thread for basting

★ Sewing thread in fawn

★ Embroidery floss or crewel yarn
in dark brown

★ Polyester toy stuffing

1 Using the patterns, cut out two body pieces from fawn fabric for the owls' fronts, two body pieces from the green fabric for the backs, and two face pieces from the green fabric.

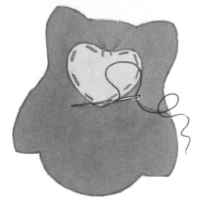

2 Turn under a narrow hem all around one face piece and baste it, right side up, to the right side of a fawn body piece with basting thread. Using the fawn sewing thread and a fine needle, neatly slipstitch the face in place all around the edge. Repeat for the other face piece and fawn body piece. Remove the basting.

3 For the two pairs of eyes, cut out four ⅜in (1cm) circles from the white material. Using the embroidery floss or crewel yarn and an embroidery needle, sew each eye in place with eight straight stitches forming an eight-pointed star, always bringing the needle up through the center of the eye before inserting it at the edge of the eye. On each owl, use the embroidery floss or yarn to embroider a small V-shape for the beak, and a line of running stitches around the face just outside the edge.

4 For the strap, cut a 20 x 1½in (50 x 4cm) strip of green fabric. Fold it in half lengthwise, right sides together, and machine stitch a ¼in (5mm) seam along the long edge. Trim the seam allowances to ⅛in (3mm). Turn this fabric tube right side out—it is useful to insert a loop turner or a "quick unpick" tool to help pull the fabric through. Iron the tube flat with the seam running down the middle.

5 Lay the strap over the face of one owl, with the seam of the strap on top. Baste in place near the top edge. Place the green back over the front, right sides together, with the strap sandwiched between them, and pin in place.

6 Machine stitch a ⅜in (1cm) seam around the edge, leaving a gap at the base so that the strap is not caught in the stitching. Remove basting. Turn the owl right side out and press. Insert stuffing through the opening in the base. Turn in the raw edges of the opening, pin, and slipstitch the opening closed.

7 Embroider two sets of claws at the base with three straight stitches each, using the brown embroidery floss or yarn. Define the wings by sewing running stitch between the wings and the sides of the body. Place the other end of the strap on the other owl front as in step 5, making sure the strap is not twisted and the seam on the strap is on top. Complete the second owl as for the first, steps 5–7.

Crib music box

WHEN MY DAUGHTER WAS BORN, OVER 30
YEARS AGO, MY MOTHER GAVE HER A SMALL
MECHANICAL MUSIC BOX. IT PLAYED A MELODY
BY MOZART, WHICH SHE FELL ASLEEP TO AS
IT PLAYED NEXT TO HER CRIB. THE MUSIC BOX
STILL WORKS, AND WHEN I PULL THE CORD
TO START THE MUSIC IT BRINGS BACK THOSE
LOVELY DAYS WITH MY BABY DAUGHTER. THIS
SOFT WOOLEN COVER WILL ENABLE YOU TO
HANG A MECHANICAL MUSIC BOX IN YOUR BABY'S
CRIB, AND IT IS PRETTY AS WELL AS PRACTICAL.
THE BUTTERFLY MADE FROM COLLECTED SCRAPS
OF FABRIC IS EMBELLISHED WITH EMBROIDERY,
AND THE EDGE OF THE COVER IS FINISHED WITH
POMPOMS, MAKING AN OVERALL DIAMETER OF
ABOUT 6IN (15CM).

You will need

★ Knitted woolen fabric from two
old sweaters, each piece at least
6in (15cm) square

★ Patterns for butterfly (optional—
see page 138)

★ Scraps of two patterned or solid
color cotton fabrics, such as cotton
brocade, for butterfly wings

★ Scrap of wool for butterfly body

★ Sewing thread to match woolen
fabrics

★ Crewel yarn in three colors

★ Contrasting thread for basting

★ Small mechanical music box with
pull string (possibly retrieved from
a broken musical crib mobile)

★ 1yd (1m) of flat woven cord in
color to match

★ Plastic ring about 1½in (4cm)
in diameter

★ Scrap of unbleached muslin

★ Polyester toy stuffing

★ ¾ yd (70cm) of cotton pompom
trim in cream

1 Draw around a 6in (15cm) plate
on each of the two wool knit
fabrics, and cut out the two
circles. You can either draw
the butterfly freehand or use
the patterns. Cut out a pair of
butterfly wings from each of
two fabric scraps, and pin the
four wings to the center of one of
the woolen circles. Slipstitch around
the edge of each wing. Cut out a butterfly
body from the scrap of wool, and pin in
place between the wings.

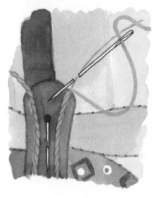

2 Use a washable fabric marker to draw two antennae. Secure the body and embroider the antennae using stem stitch and/or split stitch with one of the crewel yarn colors and an embroidery needle. To work stem stitch, bring the needle up from the underside, insert it to the right, along the stitching line, and then bring it up again halfway between those two points; continue in this way along the stitching line. For a thicker line, make each stitch at a slight angle as shown. Split stitch is similar, but you bring the needle up halfway through the previous stitch, splitting the thread.

3 In the second color of crewel yarn, embroider a line of stem stitch down the center of the butterfly body. In the third color, embroider a small circle on the end of each antenna using tiny straight stitches, and also a small star and three running stitches on each of the upper wings.

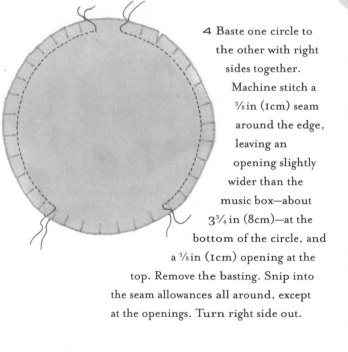

4 Baste one circle to the other with right sides together. Machine stitch a ³⁄₈ in (1cm) seam around the edge, leaving an opening slightly wider than the music box—about 3¾ in (8cm)—at the bottom of the circle, and a ³⁄₈ in (1cm) opening at the top. Remove the basting. Snip into the seam allowances all around, except at the openings. Turn right side out.

5 Cut off most of the pull cord attached to the bottom of the music box, leaving enough to tie a double knot. Cut a 20in (50cm) length of the flat woven cord and tie it to the remaining portion of the pull cord. Hand sew the knot to make it really secure. Tie the free end of the cord neatly to the plastic ring, and hand sew it invisibly to secure the knot.

6 To help stop the music box from sliding around in the woolen cover, make a little sack from the unbleached muslin by cutting out two pieces the shape and size of the music box, plus ¾ in (2cm) all around. Pin the two pieces with right sides together. Fold a length of the flat woven cord into a loop, and insert it between the layers at the top, with raw edges even; baste in place. Stitch a ¾ in (5mm) seam all around, leaving the bottom end open. Remove basting.

7 Turn the muslin sack right side out and insert the music box, leaving the knotted pull cord projecting through the opening. Turn under ¼ in (5mm) on both edges of the opening. Sew running stitch around the opening. pull up the thread to gather the edge, and secure the thread. Pin and sew the opening closed, leaving a small gap for the cord so it can move freely.

8 Insert the music box through the larger opening. Pull the small loop at the top of the sack through the small opening in the seam, and sew the opening closed, securing the loop in it. Stuff loosely with the polyester stuffing through the larger opening, so the music box in its sack is loosely surrounded and all is gently plumped up, with the hardness of the music box disguised. Turn under the seam allowances on the larger opening; pin and slipstitch the edges together up to where the cord emerges, leaving a small gap so the cord can be pulled freely.

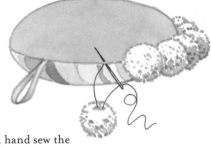

9 Finally, hand sew the pompom trim all around the edge along the seam line. Be careful not to sew through the cord at the bottom.

Hearts and pompoms garland

THE VISUAL SENSE DEVELOPS VERY QUICKLY IN NEWBORN BABIES AND THEY CAN OFTEN BE SEEN STARING INTENTLY AT OBJECTS. BABIES LOVE COLOR AND A LITTLE PATTERN, WHICH DOES NOT NEED TO BE COMPLICATED OR GARISH. THIS GARLAND OF COLORFUL HEARTS AND POMPOMS IS PERFECT TO STRING ACROSS A MOSES BASKET, CRADLE, OR CARRYCOT, AND ANY GENTLE MOVEMENT WILL CAUSE IT TO BE ALL THE MORE FASCINATING TO THE BABY. LONG RIBBONS AT EITHER END MAKE IT ADJUSTABLE TO MOST SITUATIONS.

You will need

★ Heart pattern (see page 135)

★ One 12 x 24in (30 x 60cm) piece of vintage patterned cotton fabric

★ Contrasting thread for basting

★ Sewing thread in cream

★ Polyester toy stuffing

★ One skein of matte embroidery cotton, size 4, in each of five colors (I used pink, orange, green, violet, and yellow)

★ Small pieces of thin cardboard

★ 1½yd (1.2m) of grosgrain ribbon in a color to match one of the embroidery cottons (I used pink)

1 Using the heart pattern, cut out eight heart pieces, centering any large motifs on the shape. Think about which pieces will be the backs and which will be the fronts (you will not need to consider this if you use a fabric with an all-over pattern).

2 With right sides together, baste a back and front together. Machine stitch a ¼in (5mm) seam around the edge, leaving an opening on one side for inserting the stuffing. Snip into the seam allowance on the curves and at the top point. Snip off the point of the seam allowance at the bottom. Remove basting. Repeat to make three more hearts.

3 Turn the hearts right side out; press. For each heart, push the stuffing through the opening, loosely packing it, then turn in the seam allowances on the opening, and slipstitch the opening closed.

4 Using the embroidery cotton that matches the ribbon, sew an even running stitch approximately $\frac{1}{4}$in (5mm) away from the edge, stitching through the front, stuffing, and back. (Running stitch is quick and easy to sew. Along the stitching line, just bring the needle up and insert it back in the fabric, making all the stitches the same length, small, and evenly spaced. You may be able to pick up several stitches with the needle before pulling it through, which is even quicker.)

5 For the pompoms, cut two $1\frac{1}{4}$in (3cm) circles from the cardboard. Cut a $\frac{3}{8}$in (1cm) hole in the center of each circle to form a ring. Thread a long tapestry needle with a double length of embroidery cotton as long as you can handle easily—perhaps 2yd (2m) or so. Holding the two rings together, wind the embroidery cotton around and around, bringing the needle through the central hole each time and working your way around the ring. You will need to thread the needle again but there is no need for knots to join the ends, as they will be held in place by the embroidery cotton as it is wound on top of them. It is ready when the central hole is nearly filled.

6 Using small, sharp scissors, cut around the edge between the two cardboard rings. You will need to do this a few layers at a time, as it is too thick to cut all at once.

7 Tie a length of the same embroidery cotton very tightly between the cards, using two knots. It must be tied tightly because it is holding all the threads together. Remove the cardboard circles, fluff up the pompom, and trim the pile to make an even ball. Make four more pompoms, one in each of the remaining colors.

8 Cut two 24in (60cm) lengths of grosgrain ribbon. Thread a long tapestry needle with a 40in (1m) length of the matching embroidery cotton, and tie a knot at one end. Fold one piece of ribbon in half and insert the needle through the center of the fold, then through the center of the first pompom, and then through a fabric heart from one side edge to the other.

9 Continue threading the embroidery cotton through the pompoms and hearts alternately. After the last pompom is in place, fold the other piece of ribbon and sew through the center of it. Now bring the needle and embroidery cotton back through that ribbon and all the hearts and pompoms to make a strong double strand. Finally, bring it through the first ribbon and tie the embroidery cotton securely in a knot with the original end.

Appliqué photo album

THESE DAYS BABIES HAVE THEIR PICTURES TAKEN CONSTANTLY AND THESE ARE OFTEN DIGITALLY STORED IN THE COMPUTER. IT IS A GOOD IDEA TO EDIT THE BEST OF YOUR NEW BABY'S EARLY PORTRAITS, HAVE THEM WELL PRINTED, AND DISPLAY THEM IN A PRETTY ALBUM WHICH YOU WILL, OF COURSE, KEEP FOREVER. TO MAKE THIS SMALL ALBUM SPECIAL, I HAVE CREATED A PRETTY APPLIQUÉ DESIGN FROM LOVELY OLD FABRICS, HANDWOVEN LINEN, EYELET (BRODERIE ANGLAISE), DAMASK, SILK RIBBONS, AND A VINTAGE PEARL BUTTON. THE COVER CAN BE SLIPPED OFF IF YOU NEED TO WASH IT. YOU CAN STORE EXTRA PHOTOGRAPHS OR OTHER MEMORABILIA IN THE INSIDE SLEEVES. THE ALBUM IS 5 x 7IN (12 x 18CM), BUT THE DIMENSIONS COULD BE ADJUSTED.

You will need

★ One 16 x 6¼in (40 x 16cm) piece of white linen

★ One 5 x 7in (12 x 18cm) photo album

★ Scrap of white eyelet (broderie anglaise) with scalloped border on one edge

★ Contrasting thread for basting

★ One 20 x 6¼in (50 x 16cm) piece of checked linen (I used blue)

★ Sewing thread in white

★ Scrap of white damask

★ Old lacy napkin

★ 2¼yd (2m) of silk ribbon ⅛in (4mm) wide (I used pale turquoise)

★ Pearl button

★ 20in (50cm) of silk ribbon ¼in (7mm) wide (I used blue)

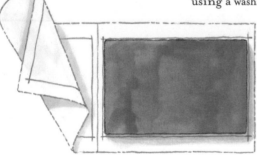

1 Fold the piece of white linen in half crosswise. On the right side, mark the center using a washable marker; unfold. Measure the closed album from the opening edge of the back around to the opening edge of the front. Mark this dimension and also the height on the right side of the fabric to indicate where the edges of the album will be, making sure the marked area is centered on the fabric. The right-hand half will be the front cover of the album and the left-hand half will be the back cover.

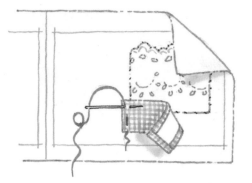

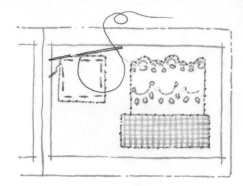

2 For the album's front cover, cut a 2¾ x 3½in (7 x 9cm) rectangle of eyelet with the scallops along one long edge. Turn under ¼in (5mm) on the two short edges. With the scalloped edge at the top, pin or baste it to the right side of the linen near the right-hand corner. From the checked linen, cut two 8 x 6¼in (20 x 16cm) rectangles and one 1½ x 4in (4 x 10cm) rectangle. Set the two larger pieces aside for now. Turn under ¼in (5mm) on all edges of the smallest piece, and pin or baste to the linen with the top edge overlapping the base of the eyelet piece; slipstitch all edges in place and remove basting.

3 Cut a 2½in (6cm) square from the scrap of white damask. Turn under a ¼in (5mm) hem on all four edges. Pin or baste in place at the top left-hand corner of the front cover; slipstitch. Remove any basting.

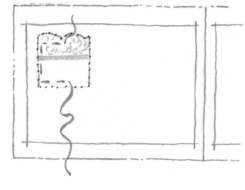

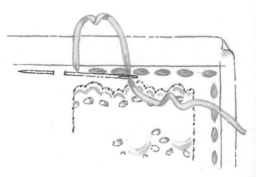

4 For the back cover, cut a 2½in (6cm) square from the lacy napkin, with the lacy border on one long edge. Turn under ¼in (5mm) on the raw edges and, with the lacy edge at the top, pin or baste to the white linen at the top left-hand corner. Slipstitch around all four edges. Remove any basting.

5 Using the narrow ribbon and a tapestry needle, sew a running stitch border around the four edges of the linen rectangle, ¼in (5mm) inside the marked edges of the book. Under the lacy square on the back cover, embroider a line of chain stitch (see Glove Puppet, step 3, page 93) using the narrow ribbon.

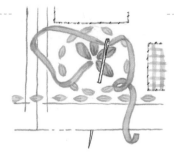

6 On the front cover, on top of the checked linen, sew on the button using the narrow ribbon and tapestry needle. In the space below the damask square, use the washable marker to draw a 1¾in (4.5cm) circle, and embroider around the line in running stitch using the narrow ribbon. Now embroider a six-pointed star inside the circle with the wider ribbon.

7 Lay the two checked linen rectangles on the white linen, with right sides together and the outer raw edges even. Turn back ¾in (2cm) to the wrong side on the inner short edge of each checked piece so there is a gap between them of 1½in (4cm). Pin the checked linen pieces to the white linen. Baste just outside the marked outer edges.

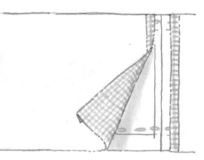

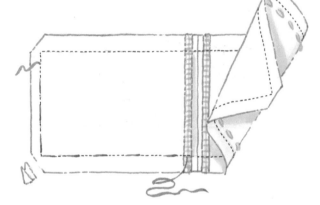

8 Check that the album will fit inside the cover, adjust the basting if necessary, and then machine stitch along the basting. Snip off the corners of the seam allowances. Remove basting.

9 Turn the cover right side out, and press. Insert the album into the linen cover. Use a damp cloth to wipe away any visible marker lines.

Bath-time washcloth

It's not easy to find washcloths in sizes and colors suited to babies, so I have cut down an adult version for this pretty 8in-(20cm-) square washcloth, made from the softest Egyptian cotton. The edges have been bound with a vintage fabric, cut on the bias (diagonally) so that it stretches easily around the corners. A small motif from the same fabric decorates one corner. You can make this project in a short time, so you may like to decorate a bath towel to match.

You will need

* ★ ¼yd (20cm) of vintage fabric
* ★ One 8in (20cm) square cut from Egyptian cotton washcloth
* ★ Sewing thread to match washcloth
* ★ Contrasting thread for basting

1 To make the bias binding, fold the strip of vintage fabric diagonally (so the lengthwise and crosswise threads match). Press and then cut along the fold. With a washable marker pen, draw a line 2½in (6cm) from the cut edge; cut along this line. You will need a long enough strip to reach around the edge of the washcloth square and overlap the end. Depending on the width of your fabric you may need to cut a second strip which you can then join to the first one (see Vintage Fabric Bib, step 1, page 64).

2 With right sides together, baste the bias binding to the edges of the washcloth square along all four edges. Ease it around the corners, creating a small fold in the binding, which can be tucked in later. Machine stitch the binding in place with a ⅝in (1.5cm) seam along each side, starting and stopping at the small fold. Remove the basting. On the right side of the washcloth square, fold the binding away from the seam, and then press.

3 For the hanging loop, make a tube 3¼in (8cm) long from a scrap of the binding (see Owl Crib Decoration, step 4, page 32).

Fold the tube in half and pin the loop to the back at one corner. Now bring the binding over to the back around all four edges, covering the ends of the loop at the corner. Turn under ⅝in (1.5cm) on the raw edge of the binding, baste, and then slipstitch the binding to the back of the washcloth. Remove the basting and press.

4 Cut a motif from the vintage fabric and turn under a narrow hem all around the edge, basting the hem if you wish. Baste the motif to the washcloth at one corner, and slipstitch in place. Remove the basting.

Carryall bag from vintage fabric

THIS STURDY AND STYLISH CARRYALL BAG IS PERFECT WHEN YOU GO VISITING AND NEED TO TAKE WITH YOU A MULTITUDE OF BABY ESSENTIALS. MADE FROM VINTAGE CURTAIN FABRIC, IT IS LINED WITH COTTON AND IS ALSO STIFFENED WITH INTERFACING, MAKING IT ROBUST ENOUGH FOR BIG LOADS. LONG STRAPS ALLOW YOU TO CARRY IT OVER YOUR SHOULDER OR HANG IT FROM THE HANDLES OF A STROLLER. QUICK AND EASY TO MAKE, THE CARRYALL IS INVALUABLE AT HOME AND IT WOULD ALSO MAKE A LOVELY PRESENT.

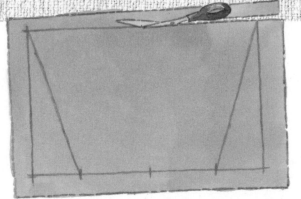

You will need

★ Large piece of paper

★ One 40 x 54in (100 x 140cm) piece of medium-weight fusible interfacing

★ One 40 x 27in (100 x 70cm) piece of contrasting cotton lining fabric

★ One 40 x 27in (100 x 70cm) piece of vintage curtain fabric

★ Pattern for bag base (see page 136)

★ Sewing thread to match fabrics

★ Contrasting thread for basting

1 First make a pattern for the main piece. Draw a 20 x 13in (51 x 33cm) rectangle on a large piece of paper. Mark the center point of the bottom line, and then mark a point on the bottom line 6in (15cm) to each side of the center. Draw lines from the top left corner of the rectangle to the left-hand point on the bottom line, and from the top right corner to the right-hand point on the bottom line. Cut out the shape.

2 Cut the piece of interfacing in half crosswise. Following the manufacturer's instructions, iron the pieces onto the wrong side of the curtain fabric and lining fabric. Use the pattern you made in step 1 to cut out two main pieces from the curtain fabric; mark the center point with a line on the wrong side, using a washable marker. For the straps, cut out two 27 x 4in (68.5 x 10cm) strips from the same fabric. Use the pattern for the bag base to cut out one base from the same fabric; cut out the notches in the seam allowance and use a washable marker to mark the dots. Cut out exactly the same pieces from the lining fabric.

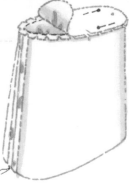

3 With right sides together, pin the two curtain fabric pieces together along the sides. Machine stitch ½in (12mm) seams. Press the seams open. Staystitch (machine stitch through a single layer) ⅜in (1cm) from the lower edge, and then snip carefully into the seam allowance up to the stitching line at frequent intervals.

4 With right sides together, pin the base to the bag around the lower edge, matching the dots marked on the base to the bag side seams, and matching the notches on the base to the center marks on the sides. Baste, and then machine stitch a ½in (12mm) seam. Remove basting.

5 To make each handle, fold over both long edges of the fabric strip so they meet in the middle, wrong sides together, then fold again and press. Machine stitch along each long edge.

6 Turn the bag right side out. Pin the ends of one handle to the right side of one side of the bag, 5½in (14cm) from each side seam, with the raw edges even. Baste in place. Baste the other handle to the other side of the bag in the same way.

7 For the lining, repeat steps 3 and 4, but leave an opening along one side of the base seam in step 4. With the lining wrong side out and the bag right side out, place the bag inside the lining, so that they are right sides together. Matching the side seams, pin the lining to the bag all around the top. Machine stitch a ½in (12mm) seam, backstitching at the handles to reinforce.

8 Pull the bag through the opening in the lining base, and turn right side out. Turn in the seam allowances along the opening in the lining, pin, and slipstitch the opening closed. Push the lining into the bag. Press, and machine stitch around the top close to the edge through all layers.

CHAPTER TWO

ACTIVE BABY

★ TUMMY-TIME RUG ★ PEEPO CLOTH ★ RIBBON TAG TEETHING RING ★ VINTAGE FABRIC BIB ★ FLOWER RATTLE ★ SNAIL AND FLOWER PILLOW ★ STRIPY BEE ★ SPECIAL BLANKET WITH TAGS

Tummy-time rug

IT'S IMPORTANT FOR BABIES TO HAVE TIME ON THEIR TUMMIES, AS IT HELPS DEVELOP MUSCLES AND ALLOWS THEM TO EXPLORE THE WORLD. THEY WILL REACH FOR NEARBY OBJECTS AND EVENTUALLY LEARN TO TURN AROUND AND THEN TO TURN OVER. THE RIBBON FLOWERS ON THIS RUG WILL ENGAGE THE BABY, WHO WILL ENJOY PULLING AT THE LOOPED PETALS. THE RUG NEEDS TO BE SOFT SO YOU CAN PUT IT ON ANY SURFACE, AND THIS FLEECE-BACKED RUG IS THEREFORE IDEAL. (IF YOUR BABY IS VERY YOUNG YOU MAY PREFER TO HAVE THE FLEECE SIDE OF THE RUG ON TOP.) THE STRIPED COTTON/LINEN FABRIC IS UNFUSSY, AND THE SIMPLE QUILTING AROUND THE FABRIC PIECES MAKES THE RUG EASY TO SEW. THE OVERALL SIZE IS ABOUT 38IN (98CM) SQUARE.

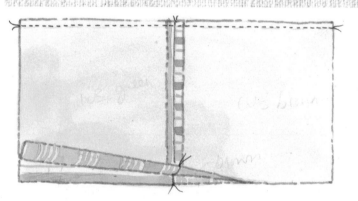

1 With right sides together and the stripes running in different directions, pin one square to a square of the other color along one edge; stitch a ⅜in (1cm) seam. Sew the other two squares together in the same way. Press the seams open. Now sew the two pairs together in the same way, so that the same two colors are not next to each other, and making sure the seams meet neatly in the center. Press the seams open.

You will need

- ★ Two 20in (51cm) squares in each of two striped cotton/linen–mix fabrics (I used a green stripe and a beige stripe)

- ★ Sewing thread to match

- ★ Contrasting thread for basting

- ★ One 39in (1m) square of white fleece fabric

- ★ Coton à broder embroidery floss, size 25, in one color (I used green)

- ★ 1⅔yd (1.5m) each of striped cotton ribbon and checked cotton ribbon, both ⅝in (1.5cm) wide

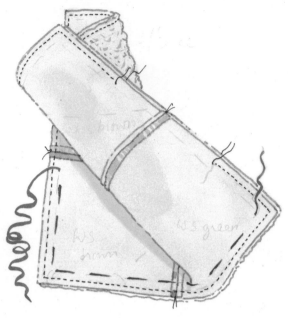

2 With right sides together, baste the front to the fleece back around the edge. Machine stitch a ⅜in (1cm) seam all around, leaving an 8in (20cm) opening. Remove the basting. Turn right side out and press. Turn in the seam allowances of the opening, pin, and slipstitch. Baste the front to the back again.

3 Using the embroidery floss and an embroidery needle, sew a double row of running stitch all around the edge. Also sew a line of running stitch along each side of the seam lines between the pieces. Remove basting.

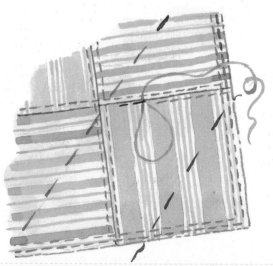

4 Now make six
ribbon flowers.
Each uses 14—
18in (36—45cm)
of ribbon,
depending on
whether it has
four or five
loops. Form one
end into a loop,
bringing the long
end over the short end.

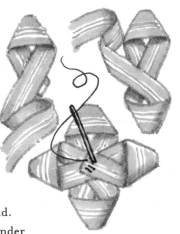

Turn the short end under
and hold. Make a second loop
opposite it, bringing the long end around to cross
the center. After making four or five loops (while
still holding them), cut off the excess ribbon, turning
under the end. Baste through the middle.

5 Repeat for the other five flowers, making
three in one ribbon and three in the other.
At the center front of each flower, embroider
an eight-pointed star (see Wise Owl Nursery
Doorstop, step 4, page 128) using the floss.
Remove basting.

6 Pin two groups of three flowers to the
contrasting patches in the rug, placing them at
two adjacent corners, so that the baby will reach
out to them. Draw a circle around each flower
with a washable marker. Using the embroidery
floss, sew running stitch around the drawn
circle. Sew the center of each flower in place,
through both layers of the rug, again using
running stitch and the floss. To make the
flowers secure, stitch behind and through the
flower. Fasten the thread securely, hiding the
end between the two layers of the rug. Remove
any visible marker lines with a damp cloth.

Peepo cloth

SURELY PEEPO, OR PEEKABOO, IS EVERY BABY'S FAVORITE GAME, ESPECIALLY WHEN PLAYED WITH AN OLDER SISTER LIKE HERE. IT IS LOVELY TO SEE THE ANTICIPATION ON YOUR BABY'S FACE, FOLLOWED BY DELIGHT AND SURPRISE WHEN THE CLOTH IS PULLED DOWN TO REVEAL A SMILING FACE. THIS PEEPO CLOTH HAS THE ADDED INTEREST OF A PRETTY SUNFLOWER FACE, WHICH HAS BEEN SEWN AND EMBROIDERED ONTO THE FRONT, COUPLED WITH A PATCHWORK BACK. THE WHITE BACKGROUND IS COTTON PIQUÉ, A KIND OF TINY WAFFLE FABRIC OFTEN USED FOR CUFFS AND COLLARS IN DRESSMAKING. THE FINISHED CLOTH IS 16½IN (41CM) SQUARE.

1 Fold one print fabric in half and, using the pattern, cut out four pairs of petals (i.e. four petals from each of the two layers). Repeat for the other two prints, so that you have 12 pairs of petals in total. Pin a pair of petals with right sides together, and stitch a ¼in (5mm) seam around the sides and top, leaving the straight end of the petals unstitched. Snip into the seam allowances on the curves, turn right side out, and press. Repeat for the other 11 pairs of petals.

You will need

★ ¼yd (20cm) of each of three cotton prints in yellow

★ Pattern for petal (see page 136)

★ Sewing thread in yellow

★ Contrasting thread for basting

★ One 18in (45cm) square of white cotton piqué

★ 3yd (3m) ribbon, ⅝in (1.5cm) wide, with looped yellow edge

★ Pearl cotton embroidery thread, such as DMC size 5, in orange

2 Make a small central pleat on the straight edge of each petal; baste near the edge. At the center of the white fabric square, draw around a plate or use a compass to draw a 6in (15cm) circle with a washable marker. Lay the 12 completed petals around the outside of this circle so no petals of the same fabric are next to each other and there are no gaps between them; pin and then baste in place. Machine stitch around the circle across the end of each petal. Remove basting.

3 Pin the ribbon around the circle, with the loops on the outside edge, covering the machine stitching; baste. With the yellow thread, slipstitch the ribbon in place between the yellow loops. Using the orange pearl cotton thread and an embroidery needle, sew running stitch along the inside edge of the ribbon.

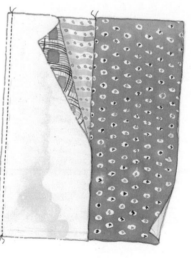

4 Draw a friendly face in the center of the flower using a washable marker pen. Embroider over the drawn lines using backstitch (see Glove Puppet, step 2, page 92) and the orange pearl cotton thread. Remove any visible marker lines using a damp cloth. At the center of each eye embroider a star with eight straight stitches radiating out from the center (see Wise Owl Nursery Doorstop, step 4, page 128).

5 Cut the remaining yellow print fabrics into three 6½ x 18in (16.5 x 45cm) strips, one of each print. With right sides together, join the strips along the long edges, using ⅜in (1cm) seams, to make the patchwork back.

6 Pin the remaining yellow ribbon to the right side of the front, with the looped edge facing inward and the outside edge ½in (1.5cm) from the edge of the front. Baste in place.

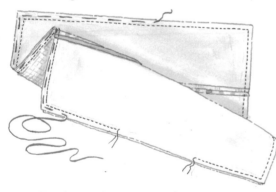

7 Pin the patchwork back to the front with right sides together; baste. Machine stitch a ¾in (2cm) seam all around, leaving an opening at the bottom edge. Snip off the corners of the seam allowances.

8 Remove all basting, except the basting that is holding the ribbon in place along the unstitched opening. Turn right side out. Turn in the seam allowances of the opening, pin, and slipstitch. Press the entire seam flat.

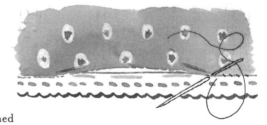

Ribbon tag teething ring

THERE IS A MYRIAD OF CHOICE WHEN IT COMES TO BABIES' TEETHING RINGS. YOU CAN BUY THOSE THAT YOU COOL IN THE REFRIGERATOR BEFORE USE, OTHERS WITH A HARD, CHEWABLE SURFACE, AND STILL OTHERS WITH COLORED RATTLES ATTACHED. I HAVE TONED DOWN THIS BLUE POLKA DOT TEETHING RING BY CUTTING OFF THE SUPERFLUOUS ATTACHMENTS AND COVERING THE LOGO SECTION WITH SOFT VELVET RIBBON. BABIES LOVE TO PLAY WITH TAGS AND LOOPS OF RIBBON, SO I'VE ADDED THESE IN MATCHING COLORS AND DIFFERING TEXTURES.

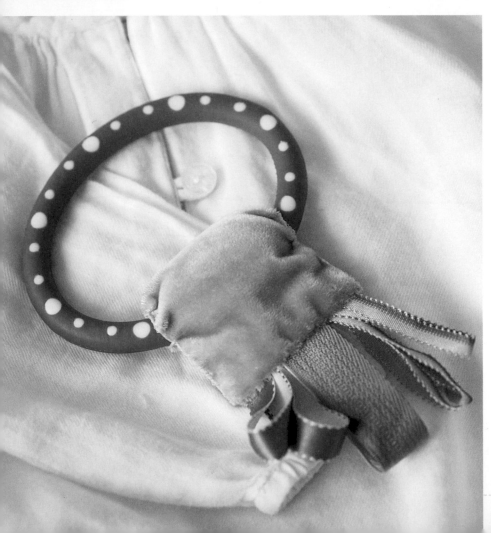

You will need

* Teething ring

* 8in (20cm) of velvet ribbon, 2in (5cm) wide

* 8in (20cm) of satin ribbon, ³⁄₈ in (1cm) wide

* 5in (12cm) of dip-dyed tape ⁵⁄₈ in (1.5cm) wide to match rattle

* Two-tone ribbon with bobble edge, ¹⁄₄ in (5mm) wide

* Sewing thread to match velvet ribbon

* Contrasting thread for basting

1 Cut away any unwanted attachments to the teething ring. Cut a 5in (12cm) length of the velvet ribbon, turn under a ⅜in (1cm) hem at each end, and baste the hems in place.

2 Wrap the ribbon around the logo section of the teething ring, matching the ends. Slipstitch the two sides (but not the ends) of the ribbon together.

3 Fold the other ribbons and the tape into one, two, or three loops, and sew the ends together with a few stitches.

4 Insert the ends of the looped ribbons into the open ends of the velvet ribbon. Baste in place. Now sew the two ends of the velvet ribbon together, stitching through the loops as you go. Sew this closure as firmly and neatly as possible as you do not want the loops to unravel. You could machine stitch it for extra security. Remove basting.

Vintage fabric bib

WHEN I MADE THESE BIBS, A FRIEND REMARKED THAT THEY WERE TOO NICE TO USE. IT IS TRUE THAT THEY ARE MADE FROM VINTAGE CURTAIN FABRICS: LINEN AND PRINTED COTTON WITH COLORED LINEN BACKS. BUT I LIKE TO SEE THINGS USED RATHER THAN LANGUISHING IN A DRAWER, AND AT ANY RATE, FOOD STAINS CAN USUALLY BE REMOVED BY SOAKING THE BIBS BEFORE MACHINE WASHING. IF YOU DO NOT HAVE ANY VINTAGE FABRIC ALREADY, SEEK OUT OLD CHINTZ CURTAINS OR PRINT DRESSES FROM THRIFT SHOPS OR VINTAGE CLOTHING STORES. YOU DON'T NEED MUCH FABRIC TO MAKE THE BIB, WHICH IS ABOUT 8 x 9in (20 x 23cm), SO THIS IS AN IDEAL PROJECT FOR USING UP SCRAPS.

1 From the solid color fabric, cut enough 1¼in- (3cm-) wide strips on the bias (see Bath-time Washcloth, step 1, page 46) to form a 1½yd (1.4m) length of bias binding. Join the strips as shown, with the seams slanting in the same direction.

2 Using the pattern, cut one bib shape from the vintage fabric and another from the solid color fabric. Place the front on top of the back with wrong sides together. With right sides together and raw edges even, pin the bias binding around the side and bottom edges of both layers; baste. Trim the ends of the binding even with the top of the bib. Machine stitch a ¼in (5mm) seam, and remove basting. Snip into the seam allowances on the curves.

You will need

- ★ Pattern for bib (see page 137)
- ★ One 8 x 9in (20 x 23cm) piece of vintage cotton or linen fabric in a floral pattern, for front
- ★ Cotton or linen fabric in a solid color, for back and binding/ties
- ★ Contrasting thread for basting
- ★ Sewing thread to match binding

3 Press the seam from the right side and fold the binding over the edge. Turn under a narrow hem on the unstitched edge of the binding, and press. Baste the turned-under edge of the binding to the back of the bib and slipstitch in place. Remove basting.

4 Centering the remaining length of binding on the neck edge of the bib, attach the binding to this edge as in steps 2 and 3. Beyond the neck edge at each side, turn under both long edges of the binding, forming ties that are the same width as the binding on the bib. Finally, slipstitch the two folded edges of each tie together, tucking in the ends and slipstitching them, too.

Flower rattle

NOTHING IS MORE TRADITIONAL AS A FIRST PLAYTHING THAN A RATTLE. A GOOD ONE WILL INCORPORATE SOMETHING TO FEEL AND SOMETHING TO SEE, AS WELL AS SOMETHING TO LISTEN TO. SIMPLE TO MAKE, THIS BRIGHTLY COLORED RATTLE IS ALL HAND SEWN. IT IS CONSTRUCTED AROUND A SMALL WOODEN SPOON—A BELL IS INSERTED INTO THE CONCAVE SIDE AND THE SPOON IS THEN PADDED TO DISGUISE ITS HARDNESS. TO MAKE IT, YOU WILL NEED A FEW SCRAPS OF FELTED WOOL OR COLORED WOOLEN BLANKETS. THESE ARE EASY TO FIND IN THRIFT SHOPS, AND BECAUSE THEY ARE INEXPENSIVE AND REALLY USEFUL, I BUY THEM WHENEVER I SEE THEM. YOU CAN ALWAYS FELT A BLANKET BY WASHING IT IN A MACHINE ON A HOT WASH, AND YOU COULD DYE THE FABRIC TO THE DESIRED COLOR AT THE SAME TIME.

You will need

- ★ Scraps of felted woolen fabric in pink, olive green, light green, orange, and reddish-brown
- ★ Scraps of T-shirt fabric in orange and green
- ★ Fusible web
- ★ Pattern for petal/leaf (see page 136)
- ★ Crewel yarn in orange, green, and yellow
- ★ Polyester batting
- ★ Small wooden spoon, about 8in (20cm) long
- ★ Sewing thread in white
- ★ Contrasting thread for basting
- ★ Small jingle bell

1 Bond the pink woolen fabric to the orange T-shirt material using the fusible web (see Rabbit Egg Cozies, step 1, page 97). Do the same with the olive green wool and green T-shirt fabric. Using the petal/leaf pattern, cut out six petals from the pink bonded fabric and two leaves from the olive green bonded fabric. With an embroidery needle, sew a running stitch border and central vein on the petals using the orange crewel yarn and on the leaves using the green crewel yarn.

2 Cut a strip of batting large enough to wrap completely around the whole spoon handle. Wrap it around the handle, and sew securely in place. Lay the padded wooden spoon on a scrap of light green wool and cut out two identical stem pieces wide enough to cover the padded handle, and long enough to reach over the first part of the spoon.

3 Place the spoon handle between the two pieces of green wool, and insert the leaves between the layers on each side, pinning them in place. Pin the two stem pieces together around the sides and bottom. Sew close to the padded handle with a small running stitch using the green crewel yarn. Trim the seam allowances to $\frac{1}{4}$ in (5mm).

4 Drawing around a jar lid of the correct size or using a compass, cut out a 2¾ in (7cm) circle from the orange wool, and another from the reddish-brown wool. Insert five petals between these two layers, leaving a space at the bottom for the sixth petal, which will be added later. Baste the two layers together around the edge. With the yellow crewel yarn, sew a ¼ in (5mm) seam in running stitch, leaving an opening between the two lower petals. Remove basting.

5 Place the bell in the center of the spoon and wrap batting around it to pad the spoon and soften the bell. Sew the batting in place. Insert the padded spoon between the layers of the flower.

6 Insert the last petal at the front on top of the stem. Pin and stitch a ¼ in (5mm) seam, again using running stitch and the yellow crewel yarn, to sew the orange circle, the last petal, the stem, and the batting together at the front. Do the same at the back to sew the back of the flower to the stem. You will need to pull the back over the spoon and to stitch tightly.

7 Use the yellow crewel yarn to embroider three circles of chain stitch (see Glove Puppet, step 3, page 93) around the front of the flower—the outside circle should be on top of the running stitch. Finish by embroidering an eight-pointed star in the middle (see Wise Owl Nursery Doorstop, step 4, page 128). If you wish, do the same on the back.

Snail and flower pillow

PILLOWS ARE INVALUABLE IN A BABY'S BEDROOM, WHETHER FOR YOU TO LEAN AGAINST AT FEEDING TIME OR TO SUPPORT THE BABY AS THEY LEARN TO SIT UP. APPLIQUÉ WITH FABRIC SCRAPS IS THE PERFECT WAY TO DECORATE PILLOWS FOR A CHILD'S ROOM, BECAUSE THE SIMPLE SHAPES LEND THEMSELVES TO NAIVE DESIGNS AND BRIGHT COLORS. YOU CAN EITHER MAKE THE PILLOW BOLD AND GRAPHIC WITH LOTS OF SOLID COLORS, OR CREATE A MORE INTRICATE DESIGN BY USING SOME PRINT FABRICS OR ADDING EMBROIDERY. ON THIS PILLOW, THE FRIENDLY SNAIL IS GREEDILY EYEING UP A SUCCULENT FLOWER!

You will need

★ ½ yd (50cm) of green lightweight upholstery fabric

★ Contrasting thread for basting

★ Scraps of cotton fabric in a brown print, solid purple, brown check, pink print, and solid gray

★ Sewing thread to match fabrics

★ Cotton embroidery floss, such as DMC 25 (I used orange, pink, yellow, and violet)

★ One 16in (40cm) square feather pillow form (pad)

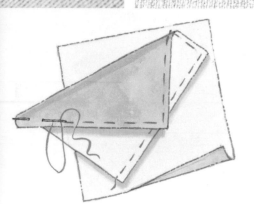

1 Cut the green fabric into two 17½in (44cm) squares. Using the basting thread, mark the seam line with a large running stitch all around one piece, ¾in (2cm) from the edges; this will be the front.

2 Cut an 8 x 10in (20 x 26cm) rectangle from the brown print. Turn under a ¼in (5mm) hem on one long edge and two short edges. Baste the rectangle to the right side of the green fabric front near the bottom left-hand corner, with raw edges even. Slipstitch the hemmed edges in place and remove basting.

3 Cut out a
4 x 5½in (10 x
14cm) rectangle of
the purple fabric. Turn under ¼in (5mm)
on all four edges. Lay the rectangle on top
of the brown print, centered between the
left and right sides and with the top edges
even. Baste in place, and then slipstitch
around all four edges and remove basting.

4 From the purple
fabric, cut a 16½ x 1in
(42 x 2.5cm) bias
strip (see Bath-time
Washcloth, step 1,
page 46). Turn under
¼in (5mm) on both
long edges and the ends; baste the
hems in place if you wish. Lay this in
a curve on the green fabric so it looks
like a stem. Baste in place and then
slipstitch along both long edges and
the ends. Remove basting.

5 Cut out
four leaf
shapes from
the brown check.
Turn under ¼in
(5mm) along all edges. Baste
the hems if you wish, and then
position the leaves along the stem and
baste in place; slipstitch all around and
remove basting. Cut some triangular
flowers from the pink print, turn under
¼in (5mm) on the edges, and position
near the top of the stem so they hang
like bells. Baste in place, slipstitch all
around, and remove basting.

7 Use three strands of the orange floss and an embroidery needle to embroider the curly stamens on the flowers in orange backstitch (see Glove Puppet, step 2, page 92), the snail's protruding eyes in pink chain stitch (see Glove Puppet, step 3, page 93) tipped with French knots (see Stripy Bee, step 7, page 77), the smiley mouth in yellow backstitch, and two lines along the body in yellow chain stitch. Using the pink and violet floss, sew running stitch outside the edges of the patches, leaves, and snail shell, and inside the edge of the purple patch. Remove all basting and wipe away any visible marker lines.

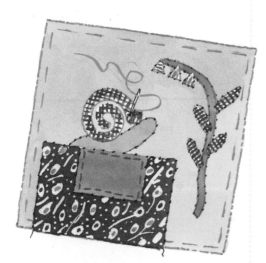

6 Cut the snail body from the gray fabric, turn under ¼mm (5mm) all around, and baste the hem if you wish. Position on the green fabric so the body is sitting on the purple rectangle; baste in place, slipstitch all around, and remove basting. With a washable marker, draw a spiral for the shell on the brown check. Cut out, turn under ¼in (5mm) on the edges, and baste the hems in place if you wish. Baste the snail shell to the green fabric so it overlaps the top of the body; slipstitch all around and remove basting.

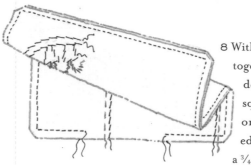

8 With right sides together, pin the decorated green square to the other one around all four edges. Machine stitch a ¾in (2cm) seam all around (you'll be following the basting line from step 1), leaving an 8in (20cm) opening on the bottom edge. Snip off the corners of the seam allowances. Remove basting. Turn the cover right side out, and press. Insert the pillow form. Turn in the seam allowances of the opening, pin, and slipstitch closed.

Stripy bee

THIS LITTLE BEE MAKES A FRIENDLY FIRST TOY. IT IS QUICK AND EASY TO MAKE—THE STRIPED BODY IS MADE FROM A RATHER CLASSY SOCK! THE BEE'S WINGS ARE MADE FROM TAFFETA RIBBON LINED WITH PLASTIC FROM A PLASTIC BAG SO THAT THEY RUSTLE WHEN HANDLED. YOU MAY LIKE TO MAKE A SMALL GROUP OF INSECTS USING SIMILAR MATERIALS, SUCH AS A BUTTERFLY, CATERPILLAR, AND LADYBUG. MAKE SURE THAT THE FABRIC YOU USE IS STRETCHY; SOCKS ARE IDEAL AS THEY COME IN MANY COLORS AND DESIGNS.

You will need

★ Striped sock

★ Patterns for bee body, head, and wings (see page 137)

★ Scraps from stretchy, loosely woven old cotton T-shirt with cellular texture

★ ⅓ yd (40cm) of taffeta ribbon 2¼ in (6cm) wide

★ Plastic bag

★ Contrasting thread for basting

★ Sewing thread to match ribbon and loosely woven T-shirt fabric

★ Stranded embroidery floss, size 25, in brown

★ Scraps from old white T-shirt

★ Suede thong 6in (15cm) long

★ Polyester toy stuffing

1 Cut the ankle section of the sock away from the foot, and cut down the "tube" so you can open it out. Iron it flat, then fold it in half. Draw around the pattern for the bee body, and cut out the two body pieces. Using the pattern for the bee head, cut out two pieces from the loosely woven T-shirt in the same way.

2 Use the pattern to cut out four wing pieces from the taffeta ribbon. Cut out two pieces from the plastic bag to line the wings. Place two wing pieces with right sides together and lay a plastic piece on top. Baste in place and then machine stitch a ¼in (5mm) seam around the sides and curved end, leaving the straight end unstitched. Remove basting, snip into the seam allowances on the curves, and turn right side out. Repeat to make a second wing.

3 Place the two wings on the right side of one body piece, just over ¼in (5mm) from the straight end, with the raw edges even with the sides of the body piece; baste. Place the other body piece on top, right side down, and baste. Machine stitch a ¼in (5mm) seam around the sides and curved end, leaving the straight end open. Remove basting, snip into the seam allowances on the curves, and turn right side out. Press.

4 For the face, use a washable marker pen to draw a smile on the right side of one head piece. With three strands of the embroidery floss and an embroidery needle, sew backstitch (see Glove Puppet, step 2, page 92) over the line. Wipe away any visible marker lines with a damp cloth. Cut two ½in (12mm) circles from the white T-shirt fabric, and position the circles on the face. With the embroidery floss, attach the circles using running stitch around the edge of each.

5 At the center of each eye, make a French knot. (To sew a French knot, bring the needle up from the underside. Holding the thread taut with your other hand, twist the needle around the thread twice, and then insert the needle back into the fabric close to where it came up. Pull the twisted thread along the needle and down onto the fabric, and then pull the needle and thread through to the back.)

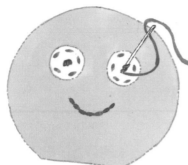

6 Cut the thong in half and tie a tight knot in one end of each length. Lay these on the right side of the front head piece, with the unknotted ends even with the raw edge at the top, and about 1½in (4cm) apart. Place the back head piece on top, right side down; baste. Machine stitch a ¼in (5mm) seam around the curved edge, leaving the straight edge open. Remove basting, snip into the seam allowances on the curves, and turn right side out. Press.

7 Stuff the head and the body loosely with the toy stuffing. Turn under ¼in (5mm) on the raw edges of the head and body openings. Pin the front of the head to the front of the body, and the back of the head to the back of the body along these openings; slipstitch.

77

Special blanket with tags

BABIES OFTEN BECOME ATTACHED TO A SOFT TOY OR SCRAP OF FABRIC, WHICH HAS TO ACCOMPANY THEM EVERYWHERE. THESE "SECURITY BLANKETS" HAVE BECOME POPULAR GIFTS FOR NEWBORNS, AND THERE ARE SOME LOVELY EXAMPLES FOR SALE, BUT THEY ARE OFTEN UNNECESSARILY EXPENSIVE. AFTER ALL, THE BLANKET IS VERY SMALL! THIS LOVELY, SOFT BLANKET, WHICH IS ABOUT 10in (26cm) SQUARE, IS CUT FROM A FINE LAMB'S-WOOL CABLE-KNIT SWEATER AND LINED WITH A WOOL PRINT. THE TAGS MADE FROM VELVET, SILK, AND WOOL OFFER INTERESTING TEXTURES FOR THE BABY TO INVESTIGATE.

You will need

★ One 11in (28cm) square of fine lamb's-wool (cut from a sweater)

★ 2½in (6.5cm) length of antique velvet ribbon about ⅜in (1cm) wide

★ Three strips of textured woolen fabric (such as cashmere and ribbed angora), measuring 2 x ¾in (5 x 2cm), 2 x ⅝in (5 x 1.5cm), and 2 x 1¼in (5 x 3cm)

★ Contrasting thread for basting

★ ¼yd (20cm) of silk ribbon ¼in (5mm) wide

★ One 11in (28cm) square of fine woven woolen fabric such as Viyella

★ Sewing thread to match lamb's-wool

★ 2yd (2m) of silk ribbon ⅛in (3mm) wide

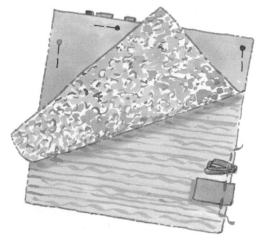

1 Lay the lamb's-wool square right side up, fold the velvet ribbon in half crosswise, and pin it to the top edge of the square about 1½in (4cm) from the left corner, with raw edges even. The folded end should be facing inward. Pin the medium-width wool strip about ½in (1cm) away from the ribbon. Fold the narrowest wool strip in half crosswise and place it ¾in (2cm) away from the last piece, with raw edges even and the fold facing inward. Adjust the tags if necessary, so they will be different lengths on the finished piece, and then baste them in place.

2 Fold the wider silk ribbon into three loops of different length. Pin it to the right-hand edge about 3in (8cm) from the bottom corner, with the folds pointing inward. Pin the widest wool strip near it, adjusting it so that on the completed blanket it will stick out farther than the looped ribbon. Baste the tags in place.

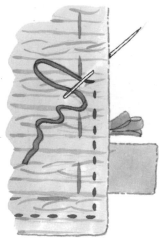

3 With right sides together, pin the woven-wool square to the lamb's-wool square, sandwiching the tags between them. Machine stitch a ⅜in (1cm) seam around the edge, leaving a 4in (10cm) opening. Snip off the corners of the seam allowances.

4 Turn right side out and press with a steam iron to flatten the seams. Turn in the seam allowances on the opening, pin, and slipstitch closed. Baste just inside all four edges. Thread a tapestry needle with the narrow silk ribbon. With the lamb's-wool side on top, sew a neat line of running stitch ⅜in (1cm) away from the edge all around. Remove basting, and press.

CHAPTER THREE

THE WIDER WORLD

★ WOOLY BUILDING BLOCKS ★ FABRIC BOOK ★ READING MAT

★ GLOVE PUPPET ★ FINGER PUPPETS ★ RABBIT EGG COZIES

★ RABBITY STUFFED TOY ★ FABRIC-LINED BOOK BASKET

Wooly building blocks

THESE BUILDING BLOCKS COULDN'T BE SIMPLER TO MAKE—JUST SIX PIECES OF WOOL FABRIC IN CONTRASTING COLORS, SEWN AROUND A SMALL FOAM CUBE, WITH THE SEAMS ON THE OUTSIDE. THEY ARE ALSO LOVELY TO HANDLE. WOOL FABRIC IS SO VERSATILE THAT I SAVE IT FROM ALL SORTS OF SOURCES, INCLUDING OLD BLANKETS, THROWS, SHAWLS, AND SWEATERS IN LOVELY COLORS AND PATTERNS. LAMB'S WOOL, CASHMERE, AND ANGORA ARE WONDERFUL FOR MAKING BABIES' TOYS, AS THEY ARE SO SOFT. WOOL IS ALSO TERRIFIC FOR APPLIQUÉ AND RAG RUGS. AND APART FROM ITS SOFTNESS, WARMTH, AND PLEASING TEXTURE, IT HAS THE ADVANTAGE OF NOT RAVELING, ESPECIALLY IF YOU "FELT" IT SLIGHTLY BEFOREHAND BY LAUNDERING IT IN A HOT WASH.

You will need

★ Scraps of woven and knitted wool fabrics in solid colors and patterns including stripes

★ Crewel yarn in matching or contrasting colors

★ One 2in (5cm) foam cube for each block

★ Contrasting thread for basting

1 For each block, cut out a 2½in (6cm) square from each of six different wool fabrics.

2 With wrong sides together, pin two squares together along one edge. Hand sew a ¼in (5mm) seam in running stitch using one of the crewel yarns and an embroidery needle, starting and stopping the stitching ¼in (5mm) from the end of the seam. Fasten the thread neatly on the inside of the seam. In the same way, add on two more squares, to make a strip of four joined squares.

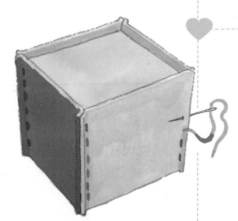

3 Wrap the strip, right side out, around the foam cube, lining up the seams with the edges of the cube. Pin the ends of the strip together and sew the seam in the same way as in step 2.

4 For the bottom of the block, pin each edge of one of the remaining squares to the bottom edge of the joined-together squares. Baste, and then sew together with running stitch using the crewel yarn, starting and stopping each seam ¼in (5mm) from the end. At each corner, sew a double stitch through all three squares at the point where they meet. Remove basting. Add the final square to the top of the block in the same way.

Fabric book

IT'S WIDELY RECOGNIZED THAT BABIES LOVE TO
TURN THE PAGES OF BOOKS AND LOOK AT THE
PICTURES, WHICH IS WHY THERE ARE NOW SO
MANY SOFT BOOKS AVAILABLE. HOWEVER, IT IS
NOT DIFFICULT TO MAKE YOUR OWN, WHICH IS
LIKELY TO BE MUCH MORE CHARMING THAN
ANYTHING YOU CAN BUY. FOR THIS APPLIQUÉ
BOOK I USED FABRICS FROM MY COLLECTION,
WHICH INCLUDES BOTH OLD AND NEW TEXTILES.
THE BACKGROUND COLORS ARE MADE FROM
T-SHIRT MATERIAL, AND THE GREEN COVER IS
CUT FROM FINE-RIBBED CORDUROY. THE
FLOWERS ON THE FIRST "PAGE" ARE MOTIFS
FROM A T-SHIRT MY GRANDDAUGHTER HAS
OUTGROWN. (THE BIRD ON THE THIRD "PAGE"
IS PICTURED ON PAGE 81.) EACH "PAGE"
IS 6IN (15CM) SQUARE.

You will need

★ One 6¾in (17cm) square of
 T-shirt material in each of
 three solid colors (I used pale ,
 green, blue-gray, and taupe.)

★ Sewing thread to match fabrics

★ Fusible web

★ Selection of scraps of patterned
 cotton fabrics

★ Old floral T-shirt

★ Sheet of baking parchment

★ Patterns for bird, butterfly upper
 and lower wings, and butterfly
 body (see page 138)

★ Pearl cotton embroidery thread,
 such as DMC size 5, in two colors
 (I used pink and orange)

★ One 18 x 6in (45 x 15cm) piece
 of lightweight polyester batting

★ One 18¾ x 6¾in (47 x 17cm)
 piece of fine-ribbed corduroy in a
 bright color (I used green)

★ Contrasting thread for basting

★ Button to match corduroy

1 Pin two of the T-shirt
squares with right sides
together along one edge.
Machine stitch a ⅜in
(1cm) seam. Repeat to join
the third square to the
opposite edge of one of
these two squares. Press
open the seams, preferably
with a steam iron.

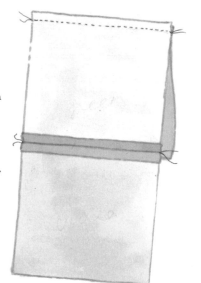

2 Place a piece of fusible web on the ironing board, adhesive side up. Lay the fabric scraps and pieces cut from the floral T-shirt on top, right side up. Cover with a piece of baking parchment so you won't get adhesive on your iron. Following the manufacturer's instructions, iron the fabric to the fusible web. Allow to cool, and remove the parchment.

3 Using the patterns, cut out one bird body, two butterfly upper wings, two butterfly lower wings, and one butterfly body from a variety of the cotton fabric scraps. If you draw around the patterns onto the backing paper, be sure to place the patterns the wrong way around, as they will be reversed. Also cut out some printed flower motifs (two with leaves and the rest without), two separate leaves, three rectangles, one bird wing, and two narrow strips for the bird's legs, from the floral T-shirt and the cotton fabrics. Remove the backing paper from each piece.

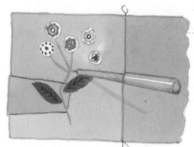

4 Place the strip of "pages," right side up, on the ironing board. For the first page, arrange five flowers and a rectangle, adhesive side down, on the left-hand square and iron in place. Iron on two leaves beneath the flowers, overlapping the rectangle. Allow to cool. Using a washable marker pen, draw flower stems running from the flower heads down through the leaves. Using the pearl cotton and an embroidery needle, embroider them in stem stitch (see Crib Music Box, step 2, page 36). Wipe away any pen marks using a damp cloth. Sew running stitch around the outside of the flowers and the outside of the rectangle.

5 For the second page, iron the two pairs of butterfly wings and a rectangle onto the middle square, in the same way as in the previous step. Iron a flower to each wing, to the square itself, and on top of the rectangle. Iron the body in place between the wings. Allow to cool. Sew running stitch around the wings, in two rows down the body, around the inside of the rectangle, and around the outside of the flower on the square. Embroider two antennae in stem stitch.

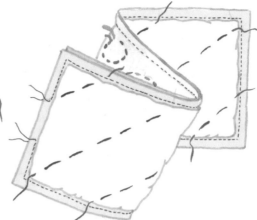

6 For the third page, iron the bird and rectangle onto the right-hand square, then iron on the bird's wing and legs and more flowers (including one for the bird's eye). Allow to cool. Sew running stitch around the bird and flower motifs and inside the rectangles. Sew two lines of backstitch (see Glove Puppet, step 2, page 92) along the bird's tail. Sew running stitch across the bird's neck but leave the eye and wing free of decoration.

7 Place the piece of batting on the wrong side of the corduroy, with the fabric extending beyond the batting by ⅜in (1cm) all around. Baste the batting in place. Place the decorated front and the corduroy piece with right sides together and raw edges even. Pin and machine stitch all around, leaving an opening in one end (the outside edge of the first page). Snip off the corners of the seam allowances. Turn the book right side out; press.

8 From a scrap of T-shirt material (without any fusible web ironed onto it), make a narrow tube that is long enough to fit around the button, plus ¾ in (2cm)—make it in the same way as the strap on the Owl Crib Decoration, step 4, page 32. Turn in the seam allowances of the opening in the book, and pin. Fold the loop in half and insert the ends into the center of the opening; pin and sew in place securely. Slipstitch the opening closed around the loop.

9 Using the pearl cotton and an embroidery needle, sew running stitch all around the edge as well as along the seam lines between the pages. Remove basting. Close the book by folding in the right-hand page along the seam line, then fold in the left-hand page on top. Using the same pearl cotton, sew the button on the opposite side, in line with the loop. (If making this for a very young baby, you may wish to use ribbon rather than a button.)

Reading mat

BABIES AND VERY YOUNG CHILDREN LOVE
LOOKING AT BOOKS, AND THIS IS AN ESSENTIAL
EARLY STAGE IN THE JOURNEY TOWARD READING.
AFTER SITTING ON THEIR PARENTS' KNEES—
WHERE THEY LISTEN INTENTLY TO A SIMPLE
STORY BEING READ TO THEM AND WILL ASK
FOR THE SAME BOOK TO BE READ OVER AND
OVER AGAIN—YOUNG CHILDREN OFTEN LIKE TO
SIT ALONE AND TURN THE PAGES OF THAT BOOK,
LOOKING AT THE PICTURES AND REMEMBERING
THE STORY. I HAVE DESIGNED THIS SPECIAL MAT
TO ENCOURAGE THIS EARLY READING ACTIVITY.
SOFTLY PADDED FOR COMFORT, AND MEASURING
22 x 19IN (55 x 48CM), IT HAS AN ENDEARING
APPLIQUÉ DECORATION THAT WILL CHARM A
YOUNG CHILD. YOU MAY ALSO WISH TO
EMBROIDER THE BABY'S NAME ON THE MAT.
THIS PROJECT COULD BECOME AN HEIRLOOM.

You will need

★ Scraps of cotton and linen fabric
in light pink, dark pink, purple,
pink check, a floral print, and a
selection of patterns in these colors
(or colors of your own choice)

★ Contrasting thread for basting

★ Sewing thread to match appliqué
pieces

★ Two 24 x 21in (60 x 53cm)
pieces of natural linen

★ Pattern for butterfly upper wings,
lower wings, and body (see Fabric
Book patterns, page 138)

★ Stranded embroidery floss, such as
DMC size 25, in taupe, mauve,
lilac, fawn, and pink—I used
three strands throughout

★ One 22 x 19in (55 x 48cm)
piece of heavyweight polyester
batting (or use two pieces of
lightweight batting)

1 Cut some uneven squares or rectangles from
the colored fabric scraps. The light pink
piece that will be at top right should be
about 6¼ x 7¼in (16 x 18.5cm); the pink
check at bottom right 9 x 6in (23 x 15cm);
the purple piece at bottom left 7 x 8in (17 x
21cm); and the floral piece at top left 8½ x
7½in (22 x 19cm). When cutting these out,
make the sides slightly uneven in length so it
has a charmingly naive look.

3 From the purple fabric, cut out an uneven vase shape, about 3¼ in (8.5cm) wide at the bottom, 4in (10.5cm) at the top, and 6in (15cm) at the sides. Turn under ⅜ in (1cm) on all four edges and baste it in place over the check patch at bottom right; slipstitch around the four edges, and remove basting. Draw the outline of the cat face freehand and cut one from light pink fabric.

2 On each of the colored pieces, turn under ⅜in (1cm) on all edges except for the one that will run along the edge of the linen. Baste the hems if desired, and then position on one piece of the linen; baste in place. Neatly slipstitch the hemmed edges, remove the basting, and press.

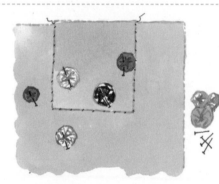

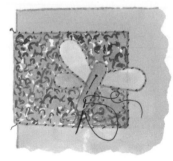

4 Using the butterfly patterns, cut out two upper wings from light pink, two lower wings from dark pink, and one body from purple. Turn under ⅜ in (1cm) on the edges, baste the hem if you wish, and pin or baste to the floral rectangle at top left. Slipstitch around the edges and then remove any basting.

5 Make eight "yo-yo" flowers (see Fabric Yo-Yos for First Shoes, steps 1–2, page 120) from the fabric scraps. Arrange them over and around the light pink patch at top right. Sew in place with running stitch using the taupe floss and an embroidery needle. For the cat's eyes, make two small yo-yos and sew to its face with running stitch.

6 Using a washable marker pen, draw the stems of the flowers between the flower heads and vase. With the taupe floss, embroider the lines with chain stitch (see Glove Puppet, step 3, page 93). Remove any visible lines with a damp cloth.

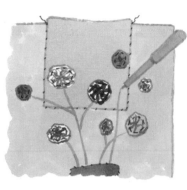

Sew running stitch around the edges of the rectangular patches, adding any other simple embroidery you wish and varying the colors of the floss.

7 Embroider the cat's nose and mouth with taupe floss using backstitch. Sew the cat's head to the purple rectangle at bottom left as in step 4. Embroider the outline of the cat's body with chain stitch and decorate it and the butterfly with a variety of colors and simple stitches.

8 Baste the polyester batting centrally to the wrong side of the other piece of linen; the linen will extend 1in (2.5cm) beyond the batting all around. Pin this piece of linen to the decorated one with right sides together. Machine stitch a 1in (2.5cm) seam around all four edges, leaving an 8in (20cm) opening on one of the short sides. Snip off the seam allowances at the corners. Press the seam open. Zigzag stitch the seam allowances to prevent them from raveling. Turn the mat right side out and press. Turn in the seam allowances on the opening, pin, and slipstitch the opening closed.

9 Use the lilac embroidery floss to sew a line of running stitches through all three layers around the edge of the mat. Finally, with the embroidery floss make a series of evenly spaced single stitches 3in (8cm) apart, through all layers, to create a mattress effect. Tie the ends of each stitch in a double knot at the back of the mat, and cut off the excess to leave ³⁄₄ in (2cm) ends. Remove the basting.

Glove puppet

BABIES ARE FASCINATED BY FACES AND ALSO
LOVE PRETEND GAMES PLAYED WHILE SITTING
ON YOUR LAP. THIS AMUSING GLOVE PUPPET
WILL ENGAGE AND ENTERTAIN AND OFFERS A FUN
WAY FOR OTHER MEMBERS OF THE FAMILY TO
INTERACT WITH THE BABY. EACH FINGER FACE
HAS A DIFFERENT EXPRESSION, WHICH HELPS
WITH MAKING UP SIMPLE STORIES AND INVENTING
DIFFERENT VOICES FOR EACH CHARACTER.
I HAVE USED A LOVELY NEW CASHMERE GLOVE
FOR IT SO IT IS SOFT ENOUGH FOR A BABY
TO PLAY WITH.

You will need

★ Cashmere or lamb's-wool glove,
  adult size

★ Scraps of T-shirt material to
  match glove

★ Fusible web

★ Scraps of white T-shirt material,
  for eyes

★ Crewel yarn or embroidery floss in
  dark brown and in a shade to
  match glove

★ Old cork from wine bottle

★ Contrasting thread for basting

★ Knitting yarn in five bright colors,
  for hair

1 To make five
faces that will fit on
the ends of the glove
fingers, draw five
ovals on the matching T-shirt fabric. For
the eyes, iron fusible web to the back of
the white T-shirt material, following the
manufacturer's instructions. Allow to
cool, then draw and cut out ten small
circles from the white material. Remove
the backing paper, and iron the eyes
into position on the drawn face shapes.
Allow to cool.

2 With the dark brown
crewel yarn or floss and an
embroidery needle, sew two small straight stitches in the center
of each eye, and sew the eyebrows, nose, and mouth in backstitch.
(To work backstitch, bring the needle up from the underside,
insert it one stitch length behind that, on the stitching line, and
bring it up on the stitching line one stitch length ahead of where
it first came up. Continue in this way along the stitching line.)
Slightly vary the length and angle of the stitching to create different
expressions.

3 Cut out the faces. Push the cork into one finger of the glove and baste a face in place on the end of the finger. Using the matching crewel yarn or floss, make a chain stitch border around the edge of the face to secure it. (To work chain stitch, bring the needle up from the underside, insert it back into this hole, and then bring the needle up through the loop one stitch length ahead. Continue in this way making a series of linked loops along the stitching line.) Remove the basting. Attach all the faces in the same way.

4 Thread a tapestry needle with the knitting yarn and create the hair by sewing a number of loops at the top of the finger, along the top edge of the face. Use a different color of yarn for each finger, and remember to push the cork into the finger as you sew.

Finger puppets

ENTERTAIN YOUR BABY WITH THESE AMUSING LITTLE FINGER PUPPETS WHILE RECITING THE NURSERY RHYME ABOUT THEM: "TWO LITTLE DICKY BIRDS SITTING ON THE WALL [HOLD THE BIRDS TOGETHER ON YOUR FOREFINGERS], / ONE NAMED PETER, ONE NAMED PAUL [INTRODUCE EACH ONE]. / FLY AWAY, PETER, FLY AWAY, PAUL [TAKE THE BIRDS BEHIND YOUR BACK]. / COME BACK, PETER, COME BACK, PAUL [BRING THE BIRDS BACK AGAIN]." BABIES LOVE THIS GAME, AND THE PUPPETS ARE QUICK TO MAKE, USING THE RIBBED CUFFS FROM OLD SWEATERS. THE STRETCHINESS MEANS THEY WILL FIT SNUGLY ON YOUR FINGERS AND, WHEN THE BABY IS A TODDLER, ON HIS OR HER OWN FINGERS. THE AMOUNTS GIVEN HERE ARE FOR A PAIR OF FINGER PUPPETS.

You will need

★ One 3 x 4in (8 x 10cm) piece of fabric cut from cuff of sweater in each of two colors (I used pink and maroon)

★ Crewel yarns to match cuffs and woolen scraps

★ Scraps of woolen fabric in three colors (I used brown, pink, and orange), for crest and beaks

★ Scrap of white felt, for eyes

I For one finger puppet, make one cuff piece into a tube by sewing up the long seam using matching crewel yarn and an embroidery needle, and fasten the yarn securely. For the neck, sew a line of running stitch 1in (2.5cm) from the top, pull up the yarn to gather the fabric, and fasten.

2 For the crest, cut two 1½ x 2¼ in (4 x 6cm) pieces from one of the scraps of contrasting wool. Snip along one long side to make a fringe. Fold the fringed piece in half and insert the uncut edge into the top of the tube. Using the yarn, sew a line of running stitch through the tube and the uncut edge of the fringe, pull up the yarn to gather the top, and fasten off securely.

3 For the eyes, cut two circles about ¼–⅜ in (8mm) across from the white felt. Place on the head, and at the center of each eye make a French knot (see Stripy Bee, step 7, page 77) to hold it in place. Fasten off the yarn on the inside.

4 For the beak, fold a scrap of the orange wool in half and cut a triangle through both layers, with the fold in the fabric on one side of the triangle. Place the folded triangle on the face with the fold horizontal. Sew in place along the fold using matching crewel yarn. To make the beak close a little, bring the two sides of the triangle together slightly using hidden stitches near the base. Repeat steps 1–4 for the second finger puppet.

Rabbit egg cozies

WHEN A TODDLER BEGINS TO EAT "PROPER" FOOD, A SOFT-BOILED EGG IN AN EGG CUP, SERVED WITH TOAST FINGERS, IS THE PERFECT MEAL. THESE HUMOROUS LITTLE RABBIT EGG COZIES CAN TURN A SIMPLE SUPPER INTO A CHILD'S IMAGINARY DINNER PARTY WITH FRIENDLY GUESTS. THEY WILL ALSO KEEP EGGS WARM AS THEY ARE MADE FROM TWO LAYERS OF KNITTED FABRIC BONDED TOGETHER—I USED FINE KNITS THAT HAVE BEEN WASHED AT A HIGH TEMPERATURE SO THAT THEY ARE SLIGHTLY FELTED. AS THIS PROJECT WILL TAKE ONLY A COUPLE OF HOURS, YOU MAY WANT TO MAKE A GROUP OF EGG COZIES FEATURING CATS, CHICKENS, AND MICE. THEY WOULD MAKE SWEET PRESENTS.

You will need

★ Fine knit woolen sweaters in two colors (I used pink and blue), felted in a hot wash

★ Fusible web

★ Patterns for rabbit head and ear (see page 138)

★ Scraps of felted wool in white, dark brown, and pink for the eyes and nose

★ Contrasting thread for basting

★ Crewel yarn in dark brown and dark pink

★ Sewing thread to match sweater fabric

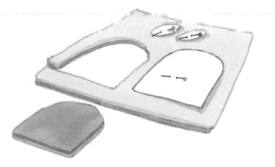

1 Cut out one square from each of the two sweaters. For just one cozy, they will need to be 8in (20cm) squares; or for a pair of cozies, 9in (24cm) squares. Iron the fusible web to the wrong side of one piece, following the manufacturer's instructions (this may take longer than on a fine cotton fabric). Remove the paper backing and place the second fabric on top of the first one, wrong sides together, with the web sandwiched between. Iron to bond the two pieces. Allow to cool. Using the patterns, cut out two head pieces and two ears for each rabbit.

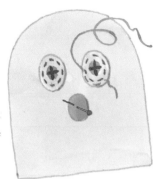

2 For each rabbit's eyes, cut two ovals from the white felted wool. Baste in place on the front of the head. Cut out two small pupils from the dark brown felted wool. Sew one in place at the center of each eye using the brown crewel yarn and an embroidery needle, bringing the thread through the center and making four radiating stitches. Finish the whites of the eyes with running stitch around the edge. Remove basting. Cut out a piece of pink felted wool for the nose and attach with a circle of running stitch using the dark pink crewel yarn.

3 Use the same yarn to chain stitch the mouth (see Glove Puppet, step 3, page 93) and to sew running stitch around the edge of each ear. The front of the ears should be in the color that contrasts with the front of the head. Pull the base of the ears together and sew to hold. Place the two pieces of bonded fabric with wrong sides together, and insert the ears in between so that the ends overlap the head by about ¼in (5mm); baste in place.

4 Machine stitch a ¼in (5mm) seam around the edge through all layers, starting and stopping ¼in (5mm) from the bottom edge. Remove basting. Use the dark pink crewel yarn to chain stitch on top of the machine stitching. Complete with a line of running stitch along the lower edge, sewing through the front only. If you make another egg cozy, reverse the colors.

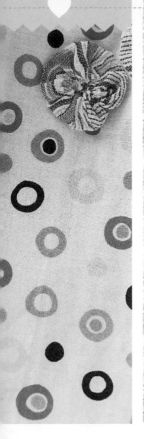

Rabbity stuffed toy

A COMPANION TO THE NEW BABY'S CATTY (SEE PAGE 18), THIS SMILEY RABBIT IS LARGER THAN CATTY SO THAT AN OLDER CHILD CAN PLAY WITH IT. RABBITY IS MADE IN MUCH THE SAME WAY, EXCEPT THAT THE HEAD HAS LONGER EARS AND THE LEG FRONTS HAVE SHOES. BETWEEN THE AGES OF TWO AND THREE, A TODDLER WILL ENJOY DRESSING DOLLS AND STUFFED TOYS, SO I HAVE DESIGNED THIS SIMPLE LINED DRESS WITH SNAPS AT THE SHOULDERS SO THAT IT IS EASY TO TAKE ON AND OFF. ONCE YOU HAVE MADE A COUPLE OF THESE CHARMING STUFFED TOYS, YOU MAY WANT TO MAKE A WHOLE FAMILY USING SCRAPS OF WOOLEN FABRIC. IF YOU DON'T HAVE ENOUGH SWEATERS YOURSELF, THRIFT STORES AND RUMMAGE SALES ARE A VERY GOOD INEXPENSIVE SOURCE.

You will need

★ Patterns for head, body, arms, legs, and dress (see pages 139–141)

★ Scraps of soft wool, such as cashmere or lamb's-wool, in three colors

★ Scraps of knitted fabric in dark pink and light pink

★ Crewel yarn in dark pink

★ Sewing thread to match fabrics

★ Contrasting thread for basting

★ Polyester toy stuffing

★ Scraps of two cotton fabrics for dress and lining

★ Two snap fasteners

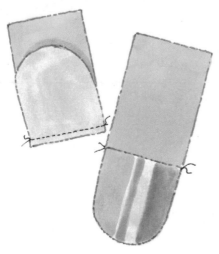

1 Cut out one body from one wool; one head, two arms, two legs, and another body from a second wool; and two arms, two legs, and another head from a third wool. Use the curved end of the leg pattern to also cut out two shoes from the third wool. Cut off an amount equal to the depth of the shoe less ½in (1cm) at the curved end of each leg in the second wool. Stitch the shoes to these legs, right sides together, with a ¼in (5mm) seam. Make up Rabbity as for Catty (steps 2–8, pages 18–21).

2 For the eyes cut out two circles from the dark pink and two smaller circles from the light pink fabric. For the nose cut out an oval from the light pink fabric. Sew these in place and embroider the mouth as for Catty (steps 9 and 10, page 21). Embroider claws on the arms using the crewel yarn and stem stitch (see Crib Music Box, step 2, page 36).

3 Using the dress pattern, cut out two dress pieces from the dress fabric and two from the lining fabric. With right sides together, pin the two dress-fabric pieces together along both side edges; machine stitch ¼in (5mm) seams. Join the two lining-fabric pieces in the same way.

4 Place the dress and lining with right sides together, raw edges even, and seams matching. Pin the dress front to the lining front, and pin the dress back to the lining back, around the top. Machine stitch a ¼in (5mm) seam, turn right side out, and press.

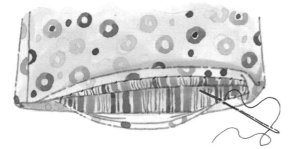

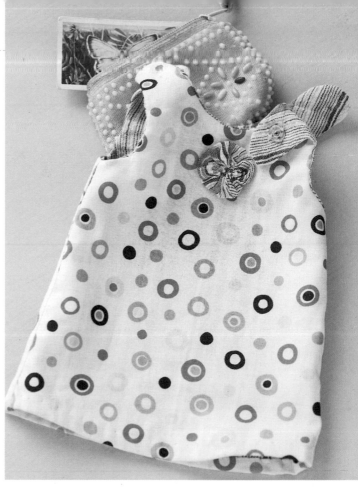

5 Cut the lining so it is ½in (1cm) shorter than the dress. Turn under ¼in (5mm) and then a further ¼in (5mm) on the dress to make a double hem, and slipstitch it to the lining.

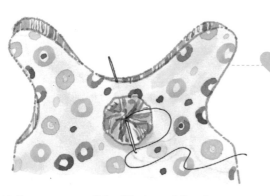

6 From a scrap of the fabric used for the lining, make a small yo-yo (see Fabric Yo-yos for First Shoes, steps 1 and 2, page 120). Sew it to the front of the dress.

7 Sew the "ball" half of a snap to the underside (i.e., the lining) of one front shoulder tab as shown, and sew the "socket" half of the snap to the top of the corresponding back shoulder tab, being careful to align them. Repeat to attach the other snap to the other pair of shoulder tabs.

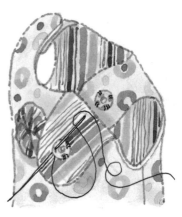

Fabric-lined book basket

EVEN VERY YOUNG CHILDREN LOVE TO LOOK AT BOOKS, BECOMING INTRESTED AS SOON AS THEY ARE ABLE TO PICK UP AND HANDLE TOYS. BECAUSE YOU WILL QUICKLY BUILD UP A SMALL COLLECTION OF BABY BOOKS, YOU'LL NEED SOMEWHERE TO TIDY THEM AWAY AFTER A "READING" SESSION. THIS WOVEN STORAGE BASKET IS IDEAL. LINED WITH CHECKED AND STRIPED FABRICS FOLDED OVER THE TOP EDGE, IT IS A PERFECT PROJECT FOR USING UP FABRIC SCRAPS—IN FACT, THE LILAC STRIPED FABRIC USED AT THE ENDS OF THE BASKET WAS ONCE A CRIB DUVET THAT I MADE FOR MY DAUGHTER 30 YEARS AGO! YOU COULD ALSO MAKE THE LINING FROM A PATCHWORK OF COLLECTED FABRICS, OR IT WOULD WORK WELL IN PRE-QUILTED FABRIC.

You will need

★ *Basket with straight sides—mine is 16 x 10 x 5in (40 x 25 x 12cm)*

★ *One piece of main fabric—I used a 30 x 18in (75 x 45cm) piece of checked seersucker*

★ *One piece of coordinating fabric— I used a 12 x 18in (30 x 45cm) piece of striped cotton*

★ *Sewing thread to match fabrics*

★ *Contrasting thread for basting*

★ *Braid trim ⅜–¾in (1–2cm) wide, and as long as circumference of basket plus 2in (5cm)*

★ *Elastic ¼in (5mm) wide, and same length as braid*

1 Cut a base and two sides from the main fabric. The base should be the length of the basket (measuring the outside) plus 2in (5cm), by the width of the basket end plus 2in (5cm). Each of the two sides should be the length of the basket (again measuring the outside) plus 2in (5cm), by the height of the basket plus 4in (10cm). The extra amounts are for the seams, for "ease" (to prevent its being too tight), and for the folded-over section.

2 Cut two ends from the smaller piece of fabric, each the width of the basket (again measuring the outside) plus 2in (5cm), by the height of the basket plus 4in (10cm). Again the extra amounts are for seams, ease, and the folded-over section.

3 Pin a side to an end along one side edge, with right sides together and raw edges even. Machine stitch a $^5/_8$in (1.5cm) seam, stopping the stitching $^5/_8$in (1.5cm) from the bottom. Repeat to join the other two pieces to these two, forming a long strip with alternating fabrics. Now pin the remaining side edges of the strip with right sides together to form a ring; stitch a $^5/_8$in (1.5cm) seam, leaving the top $^7/_8$in (2cm) as well as the bottom $^5/_8$in (1.5cm) of this seam unstitched. Press all the seams open, including the seam allowances on the unstitched portions.

4 With right sides together and raw edges even, pin and then baste the base to the fabric ring, aligning the seams with the corners. Place the lining inside the basket and check that it fits when the top is turned down over the outside of the basket; adjust if necessary. Machine stitch a $^5/_8$in (1.5cm) seam all around the base. Remove basting.

5 Turn a $^1/_4$in (5mm) hem to the wrong side along the top edge of the lining, and then a further $^5/_8$in (1.5cm). Pin and stitch close to the raw edge of the hem. You now have a casing with an opening at the side seam.

6 On the right side, turn under ¼in (5mm) at one end of the braid. With this end even with the opening in the casing, pin the braid around the top of the lining so it covers the hem stitching line. Turn under ¼in (5mm) at the other end of the braid, so it meets the first end, cutting off the excess braid.

7 Baste, then machine stitch the braid in place along the hem stitching line. Remove basting and press the lining.

8 Attach a safety pin to one end of the elastic, and push it through the opening in the casing until it emerges from the same opening that it went in. (If the safety pin is near the end but stuck inside the seam allowance, push it back a little and maneuver it around the seam allowance.) Place the lining, wrong side out, inside the basket, so the seams are against the basket.

9 Turn the top of the lining over the top of the basket, and pull the ends of the elastic until it is the right length to hold the lining close to the basket sides. Overlap the ends of the elastic at this point, cutting off the excess, and sew together. Push the elastic inside the casing. Slipstitch the opening closed.

CHAPTER FOUR

GROWING UP

★ MINI DRAWSTRING BAG ★ YO-YO NURSERY WINDOW DECORATION ★ TEDDY'S BLANKET ★ DRESS WITH APPLIQUÉ MOTIFS ★ FABRIC YO-YOS FOR FIRST SHOES ★ NURSERY LAUNDRY BAG ★ WISE OWL NURSERY DOORSTOP ★ FLOWERY PICTURE FRAME

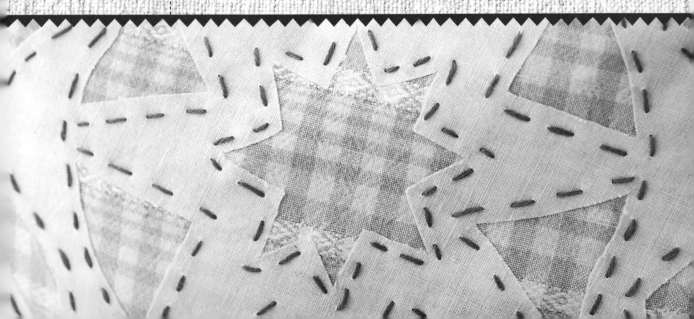

Mini drawstring bag

YOUNG GIRLS LOVE TO "DRESS UP" THEIR HAIR, AND SOON ACCUMULATE A WHOLE COLLECTION OF BARRETTES (SLIDES) AND SCRUNCHIES. AS THEY EASILY GET LOST OR PULLED OUT AND DISCARDED WHEN YOU AREN'T LOOKING, THIS DAINTY LITTLE DRAWSTRING BAG PROVIDES THE PERFECT PLACE TO STORE THEM ALL, AND A HAIRBRUSH, TOO. THIS PROJECT DOESN'T USE MUCH FABRIC, AS THE BAG IS 6½IN (17CM) TALL AND 4IN (10.5CM) IN DIAMETER, SO I HAVE MADE IT FROM SCRAPS LEFT OVER FROM DRESSES I HAD SEWN FOR MY GRANDDAUGHTERS.

You will need

★ One 8 x 22in (20 x 55cm) piece of each of two cotton prints

★ One 8 x 22in (20 x 55cm) piece of gingham, for lining

★ Sewing thread to match fabrics

★ Contrasting thread for basting

★ 1⅔yd (1.5m) of woven ribbon, ⅝in (1.5cm) wide

1 Cut two 5 x 8½in (13 x 20.5cm) pieces of the darker fabric and two 4¾ x 8½in (12 x 20.5cm) pieces of the lighter fabric. Also draw and cut out a 5in (12.5cm) circle from the darker fabric, either drawing around a saucer of that size or using a compass. From the gingham, cut out a 7 x 12½in (18 x 37cm) piece and a 5in (12.5cm) circle.

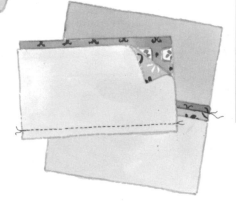

2 With right sides together, pin one lighter piece to one darker piece along one long edge; machine stitch a ¾in (2cm) seam. Repeat for the two remaining pieces. Press open the seams.

3 Now pin those two pieces with right sides together, raw edges even, and the seams aligned.

Machine stitch a ¾ in (2cm) seam at each end, leaving a ¾ in (2cm) opening in the darker portion of each seam, 1½ in (4cm) above the previously stitched seam, and stopping the stitching ¼ in (5mm) from the lower edge (the raw edge of the lighter fabric). Press the seams open.

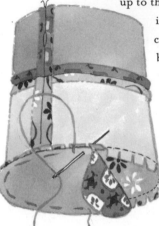

4 Staystitch (machine stitch through one layer) ¼ in (7mm) from the lower edge. Snip into the seam allowance up to this stitching at regular intervals. With the fabric cylinder wrong side out, baste the darker circle to the raw edge of the lighter fabric with right sides together. Machine stitch a ⅜ in (1cm) seam. Remove the basting and press the seam open.

5 To make the gingham lining, pin the short edges of the gingham strip with right sides together. Machine stitch a ¾ in (2cm) seam. Join the gingham circle to this cylinder as in step 4.

6 With the outer bag right side out and the lining wrong side out, place the lining inside the outer bag, so the wrong sides are together. Fold the outer fabric (which extends beyond the lining) to the inside, and turn under a hem so that that fold is even with the top of the openings in the side seams; press. Pin the hem in place. Machine stitch close to the turned-under edge.

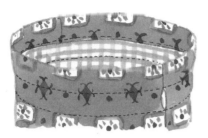

7 On the outside of the bag, stitch
a line parallel to the hem stitching line,
even with the bottom of each opening.
You now have a channel with two
openings, through which to thread
the ribbon drawstrings.

8 Cut the ribbon into two equal lengths,
and attach a safety pin to one end of one
length. Thread this into one opening
and take it through the channel and out
through the same opening. Remove the
safety pin, and tie each end in a knot,
leaving ends 1¼ in (3cm) long. Attach
the safety pin to the other ribbon, and
thread it through the channel via the
other opening. Tie the ends in knots
as for the first ribbon.

Yo-yo nursery window decoration

YO-YOS, ALSO KNOWN AS SUFFOLK PUFFS, ARE QUITE FASHIONABLE AT THE MOMENT. I LOVE THE DECORATIVE EFFECT OF GROUPS OF THEM. THEY ARE MOST OFTEN SEWN TOGETHER TO MAKE QUILTS OR PILLOW COVERS BUT, IN FACT, THEY HAVE MANY APPLICATIONS. THIS WINDOW DECORATION, WHICH COULD ALSO BE HUNG AGAINST A WALL, IS A SIMPLE FIRST PROJECT—IT IS 14IN (36CM) WIDE AND 24IN (60CM) DEEP, BUT YOU COULD ADJUST THE DIMENSIONS TO SUIT YOUR OWN WINDOW. YOU WILL NEED PATIENCE AND A COLLECTION OF SCRAP FABRICS.

1 Make a paper pattern of a 3½in (9cm) circle (or larger or smaller if you prefer). Pin the pattern to the fabric and cut around it. From the seven fabrics, cut out 35 circles in total. (You can cut two or three layers at one time if you wish, to speed up the process.)

You will need

★ Scraps of cotton fabric, in seven solid colors and patterns

★ Strong thread, such as quilting thread, to match fabric

★ 3⅓yd (3m) of ribbon ⅝in (1.5cm) wide

★ 4⅓yd (4m) of rayon ribbon ⅛in (4mm) wide (I used an antique, two-tone pink ribbon)

★ One 14 x ⅝in (36 x 1.5cm) wooden slat ⅛in (3mm) thick

★ Two suede thongs, each 3½in (9cm) long

★ Contrasting thread for basting

★ Two cup hooks

3 Cut the wider ribbon into five 24in (60cm) lengths. Lay seven yo-yos along one length, spacing them equally and leaving extra ribbon at the top and 2¾in (7cm) at the bottom. Pin each yo-yo in place, turning under the excess ribbon at the bottom. Thread the narrow ribbon through a tapestry needle, and sew running stitch through the wider ribbon and the yo-yos, along the full length. Repeat for the other four lengths of ribbon and the remaining yo-yos, positioning them exactly the same so they will line up.

2 Turn under a ¼in (5mm) hem on a circle, sew running stitch around the hem, and gather the circle tightly to make the yo-yo, securing the end of the thread (see Fabric Yo-Yos for First Shoes, steps 1 and 2, page 120). Repeat for the other 34 circles. Press the yo-yos flat, with the hole at the center.

4 Cut a 16 x 2¼in (40 x 6cm) strip of fabric. Turn under ⅜in (1cm) along each long edge. Now fold the strip in half lengthwise, so the folds of the two turned-under edges are even; press.

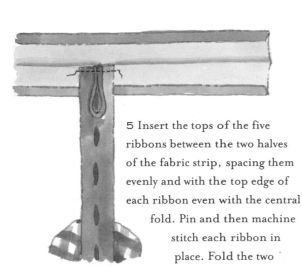

5 Insert the tops of the five ribbons between the two halves of the fabric strip, spacing them evenly and with the top edge of each ribbon even with the central fold. Pin and then machine stitch each ribbon in place. Fold the two thongs in half and pin the loops on top of the wrong side of the outer ribbons, with the ends even. Machine stitch the loops in place near the end.

6 Refold the fabric, sandwiching the loops and ribbons between the layers. Pin the two turned-under edges together with the folds even. Baste and then slipstitch to form a tube. Remove basting. Turn the thong loops to point upward, and sew in place, being careful to sew through only one layer of the fabric. (If you find this difficult, you could sew the loops in place at the end of step 7 instead.)

7 Insert the wooden strip into the tube, and tuck in each end of the fabric. Slipstitch the ends closed. Use the loops to hang up the decoration from cup hooks screwed into the window frame.

Teddy's blanket

YOUNG CHILDREN LOVE CARING FOR THEIR DOLLS AND STUFFED TOYS.
THEY CAN BECOME VERY SOLICITOUS OF THEIR TEDDIES' WELLBEING,
AND ENJOY TUCKING THEM INTO A SMALL CRADLE AT BEDTIME. WITH ITS
SILK RIBBON TRIM, THIS MINIATURE WOOL BLANKET, WHICH IS 14 x 20IN
(35 x 50CM), IS JUST THE RIGHT SIZE FOR A MEDIUM-SIZE TEDDY BEAR
OR DOLL, BUT THE DIMENSIONS COULD BE ADJUSTED. MADE FROM THE
FRONT OF A DISCARDED SWEATER THAT HAS SLIGHTLY FELTED IN THE
WASH, THE BLANKET IS DECORATED WITH COLORED FLOWERS CUT FROM
BRAID, AND WITH SIMPLE EMBROIDERY. TO GO WITH THE BLANKET, YOU
COULD MAKE SHEETS AND A PILLOWCASE, CUTTING THEM FROM THE
EDGE OF A WORN-OUT SHEET AND HEMMING ANY RAW EDGES. AS THE
ITEMS ARE SO SMALL, YOU CAN USE THE BEST MATERIALS TO CREATE
SUPERIOR BEDDING FOR TEDDY!

You will need

★ Slightly felted sweater

★ 2yd (1.8m) of silk ribbon,
  1⅜–1½ in (3.5–4cm) wide

★ Contrasting thread for basting

★ Sewing thread to match sweater

★ Three flowers cut from floral
  braid

★ Stranded embroidery floss, such
  as DMC size 25

1 Select a section on the front (or back) of the sweater and cut it away from the arms, neck, and back (or front). Mark and cut out a 14 x 20in (35 x 50cm) piece.

2 Cut two lengths of silk ribbon to fit the longer edges of the blanket. Fold the ribbons in half lengthwise and encase each long edge of the wool in one ribbon; baste. Slipstitch inconspicuously to the front and back of the wool along both edges of each ribbon. Remove the basting.

3 Cut the remaining ribbon into two lengths to fit the short sides of the blanket, allowing an extra ¼in (5mm) at each end. Encase the short sides in the ribbons, turning under the ends; baste. Slipstitch as in step 2, and remove basting.

4 Baste and then hand sew the three braid flowers to the front of the blanket at one corner. Remove basting. Draw the stems on the wool using a washable marker. Using three strands of embroidery floss, embroider the stems in chain stitch (see Glove Puppet, step 3, page 93). Wipe off any visible marker pen and press lightly with a steam iron to finish.

Dress with appliqué motifs

DECORATING A SOLID-COLOR DRESS WITH BOLD, COLORFUL APPLIQUÉ MOTIFS CREATES AN OUTFIT THAT ANY LITTLE GIRL WILL LOVE. FIND SOME LIGHTWEIGHT COTTON FABRIC THAT HAS MOTIFS WITH SIMPLE, EASY-TO-CUT-OUT SHAPES, SUCH AS THESE BRIGHT CIRCULAR DESIGNS, IN COLORS THAT GO WELL WITH THE GARMENT. ATTACHING THEM WITH FUSIBLE WEB IS A QUICK PROCESS, AND THE SEWN DESIGN AROUND EACH MOTIF IS FAST AND EASY TO EMBROIDER.

You will need

★ ¼ yd (20cm) of lightweight cotton fabric with colorful motifs

★ Fusible web

★ Sheet of baking parchment

★ Child's dress

★ Matte embroidery cotton, size 4, in four colors (I used blue, pink, green, and stone)

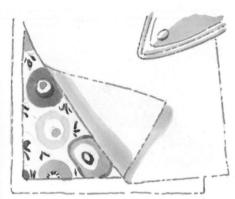

1 Lay a section of the fabric that includes about 11 motifs on top of the fusible web, with the wrong side of the fabric against the adhesive side of the web. Cover with baking parchment to protect your iron from the adhesive, and press to bond them together, following the manufacturer's instructions. Allow to cool.

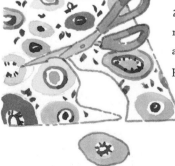

2 Cut carefully around the motifs using sharp scissors, and peel off the backing paper from each motif.

3 Position the motifs on the garment so they are not arranged symmetrically, with about six on one side and five on the other. When you are happy with the positions, iron in place. Allow to cool.

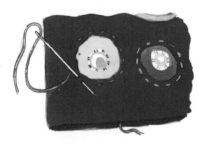

4 Using three strands of the embroidery cotton and an embroidery needle, sew a running stitch around each motif. Choose a contrasting color of thread, distributing the colors evenly. Fasten off the thread securely at the back of the fabric for each circle.

Fabric yo-yos for first shoes

FRIENDS OFTEN BUY LITTLE SHOES AS BABY PRESENTS, EVEN THOUGH BABIES DON'T ACTUALLY NEED SHOES UNTIL THEY TAKE A FEW STEPS OUTSIDE. THERE IS SOMETHING IRRESISTIBLY CHARMING ABOUT TINY SHOES. I HAVE NEVER BEEN ABLE TO THROW AWAY ANY OF MY OWN CHILDREN'S FIRST FOOTWEAR, AND SO I HAVE A LITTLE BOX OF THEM STORED AWAY IN A CUPBOARD. FOR A FIRST PAIR OF SHOES, THESE SILK FABRIC YO-YOS PROVIDE A SIMPLE BUT VERY PRETTY DECORATION. ALTHOUGH THE CENTRAL VELVET FLOWER IS MORE COMMONLY USED TO DECORATE HATS OR CLOTHING, IT WORKS WELL HERE COVERING THE GATHERED CENTER OF THE SILK YO-YO.

You will need

★ Scraps of striped silk fabric

★ Sewing thread to match silk

★ Pair of fabric baby shoes

★ Two velvet flowers

★ Coton à broder embroidery floss, size 25, to match silk fabric

1 Cut two 3½in (9cm) circles from the striped silk. Turn under a ¼in (5mm) hem on each. Using sewing thread, sew running stitch around the hem on each circle, leaving long ends.

2 Pull the ends of the thread to gather up each circle tightly. Secure the ends. Press the yo-yos flat.

3 Position each yo-yo on the front of one shoe with the gathered side on top. Place a flower centrally on the yo-yo. To attach them, bring an embroidery needle threaded with floss up through the center of the yo-yo and the center of the flower. Make stitches between each petal, bringing the floss up through the center of the flower each time. Fasten the floss securely inside the shoe.

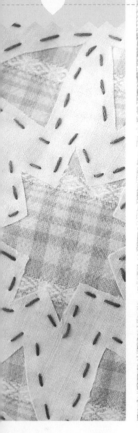

Nursery laundry bag

ONE ESSENTIAL AFTER THE ARRIVAL OF A BABY IS SOMEWHERE TO COLLECT ALL THE LAUNDRY THAT RAPIDLY ACCUMULATES. THIS BEAUTIFUL CHECKED LAUNDRY BAG, WHICH MEASURES 22½ x 23¼IN (56 x 58CM), IS NOT ONLY CAPACIOUS, IT'S ALSO A PRETTY ADDITION TO THE BABY'S BEDROOM. THE SIMPLE SNOWFLAKE MOTIF, CUT FROM AN OLD LINEN PILLOWCASE, HAS BEEN BONDED TO THE VINTAGE BACKING FABRIC BECAUSE TURNING UNDER A HEM ON ALL THOSE CUT EDGES WOULD BE DIFFICULT. THE RUNNING STITCH EMBROIDERY ADDS JUST THE RIGHT AMOUNT OF DEFINITION.

You will need

- ★ One 48 x 24in (120 x 60cm) piece of woven check fabric
- ★ Sewing thread in white
- ★ ½yd (50cm) of white linen 48in (120cm) wide
- ★ One 24 x 12in (60 x 30cm) piece of fusible web
- ★ Pattern for snowflake (see page 142)
- ★ Sheet of baking parchment
- ★ Contrasting thread for basting
- ★ Coton à broder embroidery floss, size 25
- ★ 2¼yd (2m) of pajama cord

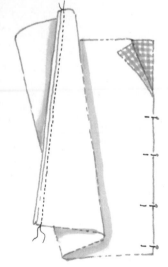

1 Fold the check fabric in half crosswise, right sides together and with the fold at the bottom. With raw edges even, pin the two layers together along both sides. Machine stitch a ¾in (2cm) seam at each side. Zigzag the seam allowances, snip into each seam allowance at the fold, and press the seams open. (Alternatively, make a French seam, which is very durable: Stitch each side seam, wrong sides together, with a ⅜in (1cm) seam. Trim the seam allowances to ¼in (5mm) and press. Turn the fabric so the right sides are together and the seam line runs along the fold. Stitch a ⅜in (1cm) seam. Press to one side.)

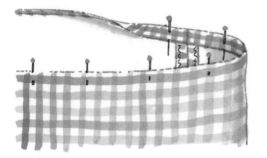

2 Turn the bag right side out and press. Turn under and press ¼in (5mm) and then ½in (1.5cm) all around the top edge. Pin and then machine stitch.

3 Cut a 5 x 48in (12 x 120cm) strip and a 12 x 24in (30 x 60cm) piece from the white linen. Set aside the long strip, and iron fusible web to the wrong side of the other piece, following the manufacturer's instructions. Allow to cool. Cut this piece of linen in half to form two 12in (30cm) squares. Peel off the backing paper. Drawing around a plate or using a compass, draw an 8in (20cm) circle on each linen square with a washable marker. Cut out each circle and fold it in half, then in half again, then fold one double-layer quarter in half forward and the other in half backward.

4 Lay the snowflake pattern over one folded circle and draw around all the cut lines with the washable marker. Now cut out along the lines—you'll need strong, sharp scissors because you will be cutting through eight layers of linen. Open out the snowflake. Repeat for the second linen snowflake. Using a damp cloth, remove any visible marker lines.

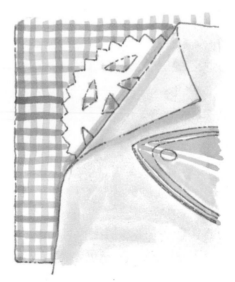

5 Place the two snowflakes right side up on the right side of the laundry bag front, 2¼in (5.5cm) from the sides and lower edge, and 2in (5cm) apart. Place a piece of baking parchment on top to protect your iron from adhesive. Following the manufacturer's instructions, iron to bond the linen to the check backing. Allow to cool.

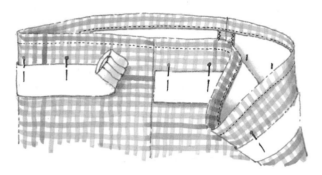

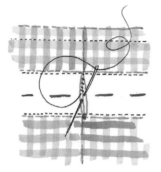

6 Fold the long strip of white linen in half lengthwise, wrong sides together, and pin the long edges together. Machine stitch a ⅜in (1cm) seam. Press the seam open, with the seam running down the center. Turn under ⅜in (1cm) at the ends of the tube, and pin the tube around the top of the bag, 2¼in (6cm) from the top, with the seam at the back of the tube, and the turned-under ends of the tube meeting at one side seam of the bag. Turn in the ends so the folds are even with the seam line. Baste the tube in place, forming a casing.

7 Machine stitch the casing to the bag ⅛in (3mm) from each edge of the casing. Where the ends of the casing meet, hand sew the ends together on the back layer of the casing but leave them open on the front layer. Remove basting.

8 Using the floss and an embroidery needle, sew running stitch along both edges of the casing on top of the machine stitched lines.

9 Sew running stitch around all the edges of each snowflake with the floss. Push the pajama cord through the casing using a safety pin, tie each end in a knot, and then tie the two ends together.

Wise owl nursery doorstop

Some parents like to use a baby monitor to listen out for their sleeping baby, but I prefer the old-fashioned method: leaving the nursery door slightly open so that you can hear when the baby stirs or wakes. To prop the door open so that it doesn't bang, this endearing owl is perfect. Not only does it have a wise and gentle demeanor, but it will sit firmly on the floor because it is weighted with split peas (safely enclosed in a muslin bag inside the body). You will need to use a stretchy fabric to make the owl, because the fabric has to be stretched to create a stable sitting position. I used knitted fabric for the back and T-shirt material for the front.

You will need

★ Unbleached muslin

★ Sewing thread in white and brown

★ Contrasting thread for basting

★ 1lb (500g) of split peas

★ Polyester batting

★ Patterns for owl body and bib (see page 143)

★ One 14in (35cm) square of T-shirt fabric in brown

★ One 14in (35cm) square of knitted woolen fabric in turquoise

★ Scraps of white felt for eyes

★ Persian yarn in brown and turquoise

★ Polyester toy stuffing

★ One 8in (20cm) square of knitted fabric with printed design in turquoise

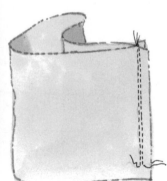

1 To make a bag for the split peas (which will be hidden, so it doesn't have to be neat) cut a 6 x 17in (15 x 43cm) rectangle and a 5 x 7in (12.5 x 17.5cm) oval from the unbleached muslin. With right sides together, pin the short ends of the muslin rectangle together. Machine stitch a ⅜in (1cm) seam, stopping ⅜in (1cm) from the lower edge. For extra strength, stitch again just inside the seam line (i.e., within the seam allowance).

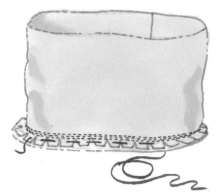

2 Staystitch (machine stitch through one layer) ⅜in (1cm) from the lower edge, and then snip into the seam allowance up to the stitching all around. Now pin and baste the lower edge to the oval, right sides together, and stitch a ½in (12mm) seam. Stitch again just inside the seam line. Remove basting and turn right side out.

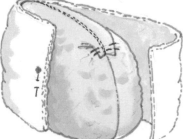

3 Fill the muslin bag with the split peas. Pin the top edges together, and machine stitch a ⅜in (1cm) seam. Stitch again just inside the seam line. Turn over the corners and baste them down. Wrap batting around the bag of peas, and baste the edges together.

4 Using the body pattern, cut one front from the brown T-shirt fabric and one back from the turquoise knitted fabric. For the eyes, cut two circles from the white felt and pin them onto the front near the top. Attach using one strand of the brown Persian yarn and an embroidery needle to sew running stitch around the edges. Make an eight-pointed star in the middle of each eye, using straight stitches and bringing the needle through the center with each stitch.

5 Draw on the eyebrows and beak with a washable marker. Using one strand of the turquoise yarn, sew over the line with stem stitch (see Crib Music Box, step 2, page 36). With a damp cloth remove any visible marker lines.

6 With right sides together, pin the front to the back. Stitch a ⅜ in (1cm) seam all around the edges, leaving an opening along the base large enough to insert the bag of split peas. Snip off the corners of the seam allowances, snip into the seam allowances on the curves, and turn right side out.

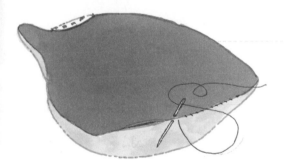

7 Stuff the head and the top of the body with the toy stuffing, pushing it firmly into the tips of the ears. Insert the bag of peas and add stuffing all around the bag to mask its shape. Finally add some pieces of the batting between the outside fabric and the stuffing to create a smooth, even surface. Pull the opening at the base together, stretching the fabric. Turn in the seam allowances, pin, and baste. Check that the owl will sit squarely on the base, and adjust if necessary, then slipstitch the opening.

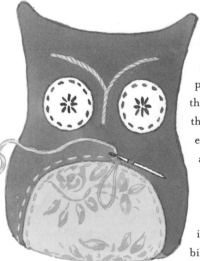

8 Use the bib pattern to cut a single piece of the printed wool. Place the bib on the front of the owl so the straight edge matches the seam at the base. Attach with running stitch in the turquoise Persian yarn just inside the edge of the bib. Follow the outline with a second line of running stitch just outside the bib.

Flowery picture frame

FROM THE MASSES OF PHOTOGRAPHS YOU WILL ACCUMULATE IN THE EARLY YEARS OF YOUR CHILD'S LIFE, YOU ARE BOUND TO HAVE FAVORITES THAT YOU'LL WANT TO DISPLAY IN A SPECIAL FRAME. IT DOESN'T HAVE TO BE SILVER OR ANTIQUE OR EVEN EXPENSIVE—A HOMEMADE FRAME CAN BE BEAUTIFUL AND IT WILL, OF COURSE, BE UNIQUE. THIS CHARMING PICTURE FRAME, WHICH HAS AN OPENING THE SIZE OF A STANDARD 4 x 6IN (10 x 15CM) PHOTOGRAPH, HAS BEEN MADE FROM SCRATCH USING A PIECE OF STIFF CARDBOARD PADDED WITH BATTING AND COVERED WITH FABRIC. THE FABRIC NEEDS TO BE SLIGHTLY STRETCHY SO THAT YOU CAN PULL THE CUT EDGES AROUND THE CENTRAL OPENING. HERE I HAVE USED A VERY FINE-RIBBED CORDUROY IN CREAM.

You will need

- ★ One 8¼ x 11¾in (21 x 29.7cm, or size A4) piece of firm cardboard

- ★ One 4 x 6in (10 x 15cm) piece of posterboard (thin card), to use as pattern

- ★ One 10½ x 14in (27 x 36cm) piece of polyester batting

- ★ Double-sided tape

- ★ Two 10½ x 14¼in (27 x 36cm) pieces of fine-ribbed corduroy

- ★ Sewing thread to match corduroy

- ★ Pattern for flower (see page 135)

- ★ Scraps of T-shirt material in assorted colors

- ★ Ten small velvet flowers in assorted colors

- ★ Coton à broder size 25 embroidery floss in one color

- ★ 20in (50cm) of elastic, ⅛in (3mm) wide

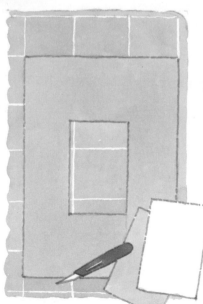

I Place the piece of cardboard on a cutting mat, and position the piece of posterboard on top, at the center of the cardboard. Draw around the posterboard, and cut out the rectangular hole using a craft knife.

2 Lay the cardboard centrally on the piece of batting. Stick double-sided tape all around the inner and outer edges of the cardboard, and bring the batting over onto the tape to secure it around the outer edge. Cut an X-shape in the batting between the corners of the central opening, and bring the resulting triangles over onto the tape to secure them around the inner edge.

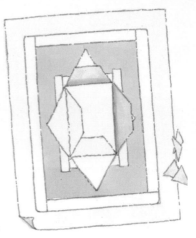

3 Lay the cardboard, padded side down, centrally on the wrong side of one of the pieces of corduroy. Cut an X-shape in the corduroy between the corners of the opening, and cut away the points of the triangles so that approximately $1\frac{1}{4}$in (3cm) of corduroy is left to stretch around to the back of the cardboard.

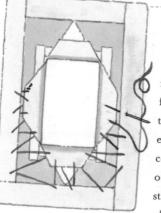

4 Pull the corduroy over the inner and outer edges of the frame and, using the sewing thread, sew each inner edge to the corresponding outer edge of the corduroy. Use large stitches and pull the two sides of the fabric together tightly so that the cover is even and smooth. (To make the corners flat, you could miter them. Unfold the edges adjacent to the corner, and fold the corner diagonally so that the fold lines from the adjacent sides line up. Trim off the triangle between these fold lines, and then refold each side, forming a miter at the corner, which you slipstitch.)

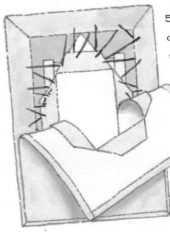

5 Center the other piece of corduroy, right side up, over the back of the frame. Turn under the excess fabric around the edge and neatly slipstitch to the corduroy underneath, using matching sewing thread. Make cuts for the central opening as in step 3, but instead of pulling the excess fabric through the opening, simply turn it under on each edge. Slipstitch to the corduroy beneath, taking particular care at the corners.

6 Using the flower pattern, cut out ten flowers from the T-shirt fabric. Pinch together the base of each flower and secure with a couple of stitches, and then fasten off the thread.

7 Pair up the T-shirt fabric flowers with contrasting velvet flowers, placing the velvet flowers on top. Arrange the pairs evenly on the front of the frame. Using the floss and an embroidery needle, attach each pair of flowers to the front of the frame with straight stitches forming a star shape through the center and between the petals. Finish off neatly and firmly at the back of each pair.

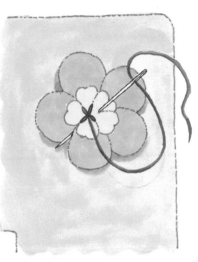

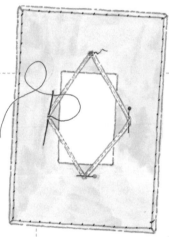

8 With the same floss, embroider blanket stitch all around the inner and outer edges of the frame. (To work blanket stitch, bring the needle out on the edge, insert it one stitch length in from that point and a little farther along, then bring it out on the edge directly opposite where it went in, with the needle on top of the loop formed by the floss. Continue in this way along the edge, keeping the size of the stitches the same.)

9 On the back of the frame, pin the ends of the length of elastic together at center top, about ⅜in (1cm) from the inner edge. Divide this loop into quarters and pin these points at the center of each side and of the bottom, ⅜in (1cm) from the inner edge, forming a diamond shape. If the elastic is not quite taut enough, adjust the length, and repin. Using the floss, sew the elastic securely to the fabric at these four points. This will hold the photo in place and make it easy to change.

CATTY
STUFFED TOY
(SEE PAGE 18)

These templates are shown at their actual size, so please photocopy them at 100%.

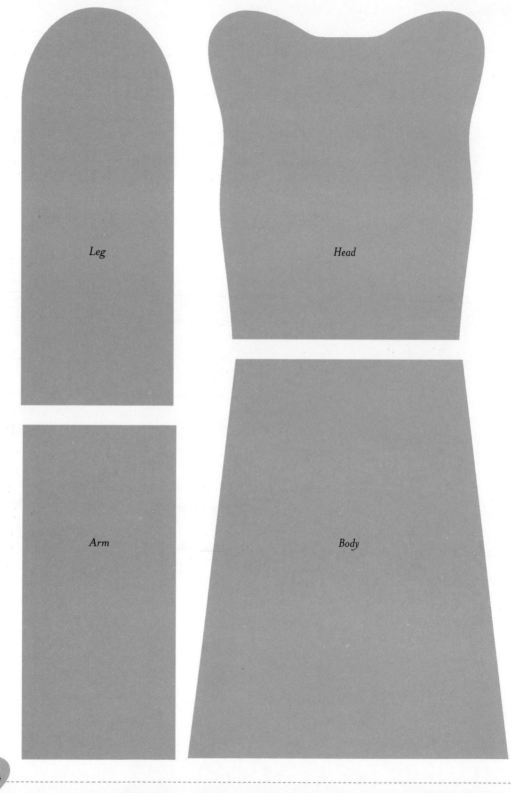

Leg

Head

Arm

Body

Face

Body

OWL CRIB DECORATION
(SEE PAGE 30)

These templates are shown at their actual size, so please photocopy them at 100%.

HEARTS AND POMPOMS GARLAND
(SEE PAGE 38)

This template is shown at half its actual size, so please photocopy it at 200%.

FLOWERY PICTURE FRAME
(SEE PAGE 130)

This pattern is shown at its actual size, so please photocopy it at 100%.

CARRYALL BAG FROM VINTAGE
FABRIC (SEE PAGE 48)

*This pattern is shown at half its actual size,
so please photocopy it at 200%.*

FLOWER RATTLE
(SEE PAGE 66)

*This pattern is shown at its
actual size, so please photocopy
it at 100%.*

PEEPO CLOTH
(SEE PAGE 58)

*This pattern is shown at its
actual size, so please
photocopy it at 100%.*

STRIPY BEE (SEE PAGE 74)

These patterns are shown at their actual size,
so please photocopy them at 100%.

VINTAGE FABRIC BIB (SEE PAGE 64)

This pattern is shown at half its actual size, so please
photocopy it at 200%.

Body

Head

Wing

FABRIC BOOK (SEE PAGE 84)

These patterns are shown at their actual size,
so please photocopy them at 100%.

Butterfly body

Butterfly upper wing

Butterfly lower wing

Bird

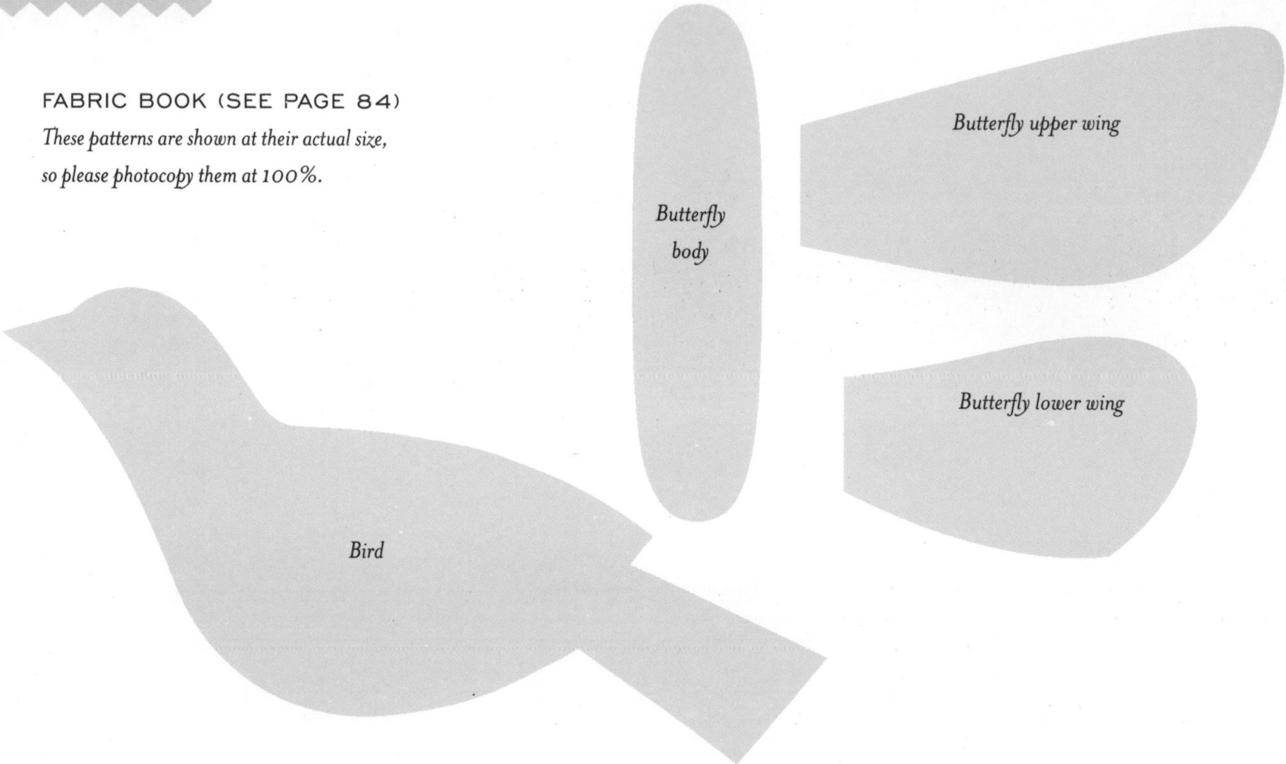

RABBIT EGG COZIES (SEE PAGE 96)

These patterns are shown at their actual size, so please
photocopy them at 100%.

Ear

Head

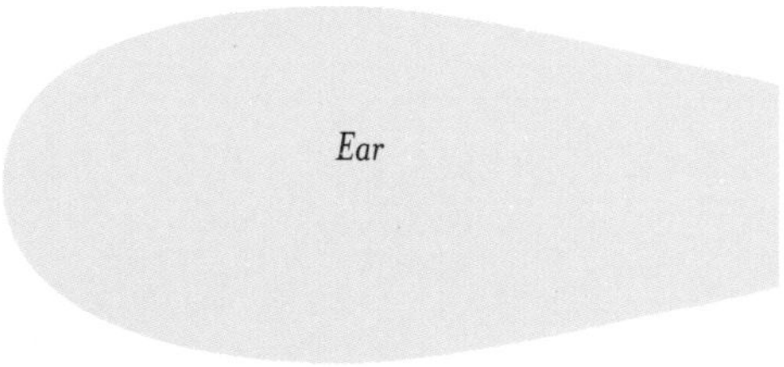

RABBITY STUFFED TOY (SEE PAGE 98)

These patterns are shown at their actual size, so please photocopy them at 100%. There are more Rabbity patterns on pages 140—141.

Leg

Head

Arm

Body

Dress

NURSERY LAUNDRY BAG
(SEE PAGE 122)

This pattern is shown at its actual size,
so please photocopy it at 100%.

BIRD MOBILE (SEE PAGE 14)

This template is shown at its actual size, so
please photocopy it at 100%.

WISE OWL NURSERY DOORSTOP (SEE PAGE 126)

These patterns are shown at half their actual size,
so please photocopy them at 200%.

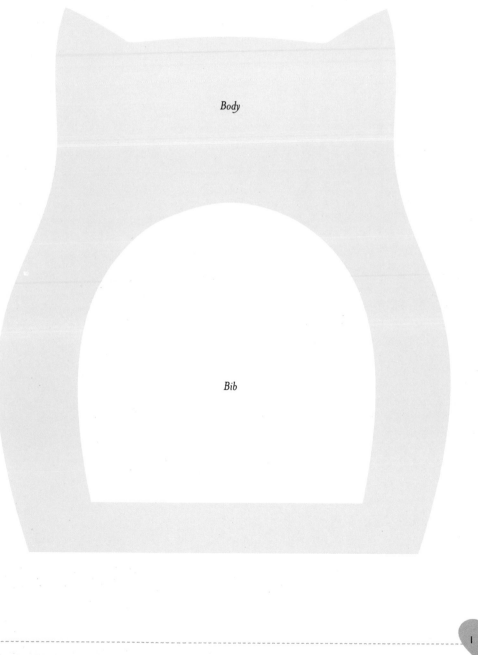

Body

Bib

ACKNOWLEDGMENTS

I would like to thank my publisher, Cindy Richards, for taking on my ideas and enthusiasms and for commissioning this book. Many thanks to Alison Wormleighton for her clear and seamless editing and to Kate Simunek for the lovely step-by-step drawings. As always, special thanks are due to Gillian Haslam for her consistent support and encouragement throughout this project.

Two brilliant needlecraft sources I used for this book:
www.beyond-fabrics.com for fabrics, notions (haberdashery), books, and ideas
www.londonbeadco.co.uk for embroidery threads and notions, especially silk ribbons